Rose E. Hlavka-Fluhrer

SOME PATHS ARE MADE TO BE TAKEN___

I HEARD A CALL...

AND I ANSWERED IT!

Rose E. Hlavka-Fluhrer

RED CLOVER PRESS

TRAVERSE CITY, MICHIGAN

SOME PATHS ARE MADE TO BE TAKEN - - -

I heard a Call . . . and I answered it!

Copyright © 1995 by Rose E. Hlavka-Fluhrer

All rights reserved. For information address: Red Clover Press, 12780 So. Regal St., Traverse City, Michigan 49684-5342

Library of Congress Cataloging-in-Publication Data

Hlavka-Fluhrer, Rose E.

   Some paths are made to be taken - - -

      I heard a Call . . . And I answered it!

  ISBN #0-9646859-0-6

Additional copies of this book may be ordered by sending $6.95 plus tax (for MI residents) + $2.00 postage & handling to: Red Clover Press, 12780 So. Regal St., Traverse City, Michigan 49684-5342. Tel: 616-947-2285

Printed in the United States of America

FOREWORD

I heard a Call . . . and I answered it!

In grade school, I was always sketching. A picture of a nurse wearing a cap and uniform; carrying a tray holding a glass of water and medicine to a patient in bed seemed to be my favorite. Little did I realize then that my inner thoughts would come true for me.

Within the next thirty-five years, while my children were still in high school, I entered nurse's training, graduated and received employment at local hospitals. After my husband's death, I received an invitation; a Call I did not understand. As rewarding as my nursing career was to me, I felt I was called to leave my home and assist those less fortunate than myself in a corner of America about which I knew nothing.

I had to make a decision: continue my nursing career or pack my bags to be away for a year (or more). My most important decision was not what but when. Before long, I found myself on a plane bound for VISTA Volunteer training in Boston. The Call I heard was beginning to take shape for me. I was to learn that sometimes we can do no more than stand with the poor. They prize things such as a kind word, gentleness, compassion and listening to their sorrows. Our very presence can make a difference.

For several years following my VISTA service, I considered the idea of writing a book about my experiences.

I continued to recall a remark made to me by Ed Goodhouse, my VISTA supervisor, "Rose, why don't you write a book?" Other projects, however, seemed to get in the way and writing the book was placed on the 'back burner.' The more I thought about it, the more I knew it was something I had to do to pay tribute to all the wonderful people of Bridgewater and Woodstock, Vermont, and surrounding areas and also the people of Ogemaw, Iosco, Arenac and Oscoda Counties, Michigan, with whom I have had the honor to work and to serve.

I knew, somewhere out there, someone is waiting to hear how to share a part of their life assisting those who need a helping hand.

One day I asked myself, "Rose, how much longer before the book will become reality?" The answer came to me, "To live is to respond to God's Call in love and mercy and to thank Him for the courage to deal with these scientific experiences." This book is the answer to the question.

This book is dedicated to the memory of Edward W. Goodhouse, University of Vermont Co-operative Extension Service agent for Youth of Woodstock, Vermont. Ed was my friend, my counselor, my support . . . my immediate VISTA supervisor. He extended his kindness and understanding in my attempts to assist the underprivileged of Windsor County, Vermont, as I pored out my frustrations and problems. My one regret is that Ed cannot be here to enjoy this book now . . . with you.

I also say 'thank you' from the bottom of my heart for the warm welcome I received upon my arrival in the communities where I worked as a VISTA, for accepting the projects we worked on together and the opportunity to be with them during some really tough times. I feel I have received far more than I have ever given.

I offer my deepest gratitude, especially, to the children and young folk, who captivated my life so many years ago.

This bit of verse by Ellen P. Allerton from BEAUTIFUL THINGS is dedicated to them:

"Beautiful faces are those that wear,

It matters little if dark or fair.

Whole-souled honesty printed there!"

I extend my love and appreciation to my children, Judy, Tom and Nancy, for their patience and understanding while their mother struggled with decisions in my Call to leave home to assist the needy in some remote corner of America. I also wish to extend my deepest gratitude to my daughter, Nancy, for assisting me in bringing my book to completion. I thank my friend Edmund, who offered encouragement while I attempted to bring my story to reality.

One hundred percent of the proceeds from the sale of this book will assist children's and families' organizations in Windsor County, Vermont, and Ogemaw County,

Michigan, and to Habitat for Humanity, Grand Traverse Region, Michigan, my home State.

Acknowledgment is made to Abbey Press, St. Meinrad, Indiana, for permission in using their cover for my book.

CONTENTS

Pages

I   DECISIONS 1

"And I said to the angel who stood at the gate of the year, 'Give me light that I may tread safely into the unknown.' And the angel replied, 'Go out into the darkness and put your hand into the hand of God. That shall be to you better than a light and safer than a known way.'"

II   UNEXPECTED EXPERIENCES 9

"I shall pass through this world but once. Any good, therefore, that I can do or any kindness that I can show to my fellowman, let me not defer nor neglect it . . . for I shall not pass this way again"

III	<u>DO UNTO OTHERS</u>	17

"You must have faith beyond faith . . . to the point you believe your faith will move a mountain."

IV	<u>I LIFT UP MINE EYES TO THE HILLS</u> . . .	35

Lift me, O God above myself, that I may understand the needs of others; in this challenging year ahead.

V	<u>PEOPLE HELPING PEOPLE</u>	49

I can do all things in him who strengthens me.

VI	<u>SO LONG AS WE LOVE, WE SERVE</u>	61

"You cannot do a kindness too soon, for you never know how soon it will be too late."

VII	<u>". . . A MAN'S REACH SHOULD EXCEED HIS GRASP"</u>	77

"No man is an island, entire of itself; every man is a piece of the continent; a part of the main . . ."

| VIII | A STRANGER'S EYES SEE THE CLEAREST . . . . 89 |

"Though we travel the world over to find the beautiful, we must carry it with us or we find it not."

Unknown

| IX | GROW WHERE YOU ARE PLANTED . . . 99 |

"Ask not what your country can do for you ... but ask what you can do for your country."

President John Fitzgerald Kennedy
in his inaugural address

| X | THE GRAND OL' PATRIARCH . . . . . . 111 |

"It is not I who speaks, but life within me who has much to say"

| XI | SAND FLEAS AND WILD ANIMALS . . . . 121 |

A part of wisdom is to know the value of now ... before it is gone forever.

XII	<u>A HAPPY VISTA</u>	131

> Whatever hour you are blessed with, take it with grateful hands.

XIII	<u>VERMONT'S BLACKBERRIES</u>	145

> "Whose woods these are . . . I think
> I know,
> His house is in the village,
> though.
> He will not see me standing there
> To watch his woods fill up with snow."
>
>   Robert Frost

XIV	<u>I WAS A STRANGER</u>	155

> "It isn't what happens to you, but . . . how you handle it that counts.

XV	<u>WHEN THE RIPPLES REACHED ANOTHER SHORE</u>	165

> "What, giving again?" I ask in dismay, "And must I keep giving and giving away?" "Oh no," said the angel, piercing me through. "Just give until God stops giving to you."

XVI   THE LAST FAREWELL 179

"There are plateaus to achievement in everyone's life. Pauses when we can stop, briefly, to re-assess our progress. But, there is no end to what anyone can accomplish."

XVII   SOME PATHS ARE MADE TO BE TAKEN - - -
I HEARD A CALL . . .
AND I ANSWERED IT! 187

God's work <u>must</u> truly be our own.

CHAPTER I

DECISIONS

"And I said to the angel who stood at the gate of the year, 'Give me light that I may tread safely into the unknown.' And he replied, 'Go out into the darkness and put your hand into the hand of God. That shall be to you better than a light and safer than a known way.'"

Have you ever packed a bag to be away from home for a year? Not knowing where the year would take you? I was about to begin a journey. . . a journey into the unknown that would prove to be the most memorable, fascinating and exciting time I have ever known. I was heading for Boston to begin a six-week training period in preparation of becoming a VISTA volunteer. . . a Volunteer In Service To America, the domestic Peace Corps.

Imagine, if you can, just two weeks ago you packed away your uniform and cap, put away your instruments as a nurse, sold your car and you didn't know, at this time of your life, if you would be back to your job or to your city. In fact, you suspected your entire future would be changed, reshaped to fit the more urgent needs, not your selfish needs, but the growing needs of others.

Life has been good. I worked as a nurse at the two local hospitals: Munson Medical Center and Traverse City Osteopathic Hospital, respectively, having received my certification a few years before and feeling a true calling to "bear one another's burdens."

Before my decision to join VISTA, newspapers, radio and television headlines blared: JOIN VISTA AND SEE THE WORLD. IT MAY LOOK A LITTLE DIFFERENT WHEN YOU'RE THROUGH.

I didn't really understand what they were talking about. Then I heard a voice. "You care about what happens to those in need and they care enough to try to do something about it. Your place is with them. Through choice, you will live with the poor under conditions *they* did not choose."

As volunteering was my 'middle name,' I volunteered to assist at church and school activities, as a Girl Scout leader, 4-H leader and as an American Red Cross Gray Lady at the Traverse City State Hospital, where I read to, walked and visited with, wrote letters for and assisted the patients with various needs. The cliche 'the busiest mothers are always the first to be called upon' certainly applied to me. After my husband died, I knew somewhere out there was a time and place for me to do something more and VISTA was the path I was to take to help those less fortunate than myself. It seemed only natural that I continue to do for others and to seek out their needs.

What is VISTA? Volunteers In Service To America or the Domestic Peace Corps, one of the major anti-poverty programs established by the Economic Opportunity Act of nineteen sixty-four. The idea of a Domestic Peace Corps originated in nineteen sixty-two when President J.F. Kennedy appointed a task force to study the feasibility of recruiting volunteers to help the poor in the United States. The task force, including members of the Cabinet, worked for a year to set up what they came to call the National Service Corps. In nineteen sixty-three, the National Service Corps legislation passed the Senate but the bill never came to a vote in the House. Following the death of President Kennedy, President Lyndon B. Johnson established a task force to draw up proposals for what would become the Economic Opportunity Act, including a section on Volunteers of America. Not to be confused with the Salvation Army's Volunteers of America, the name was changed to Volunteers In Service To America or VISTA.

VISTA really began on February twenty-sixth, nineteen sixty-five when nineteen volunteers completed the first training program conducted by the Florida Institute of continuing Studies in St. Petersburg and were awarded their graduation certificates by Mrs. Lyndon B. Johnson. They served in all fifty States, the District of Columbia, Puerto Rico, the Virgin Islands and American Samoa. VISTA offered an opportunity for men and women from all economic, geographic and social groups to participate in the Nation's War on Poverty. Volunteers served where they were requested and needed. They were assigned to Appalachia, rural areas, urban slums, small towns and large cities, migrant camps, Indian reservations, agencies concerned with the mentally handicapped, Foster Grandparents, Head Start and Job Corps. The minimum age limit was eighteen; there was no maximum age limit or special education requirements. There were retirees and young people with college degrees and high school graduates. Married couples were to join together and be placed together in their assignment and could not have dependents under eighteen.

The VISTA application included seven pages seeking information regarding personal and work assignment preferences, medical history, driver status, legal history, education, military service, foreign language ability, acquired skills, teaching and tutoring training, employment and job references and six personal and employment references.

The Evaluation and Placement Division attempted to select volunteers from applications of varied experiences and backgrounds, who, having a sincere desire to help others, could perform effectively. Their past experience had to indicate an awareness of social problems and empathy toward the less fortunate. They had to show an active participation in youth groups, social service organizations and evidence of stability in their work history. They had to show ability to guide others in new and changing situations.

When I received the VISTA application, I placed it on my desk and glanced at it every few days; trying to convince myself that for a forty-five-year-old nurse, at the height of her career, the idea of VISTA service was impractical and pure nonsense! I learned that VISTA expects its volunteers to live at the level of the people with whom they would be working and they wouldn't get much money. Did I possess the courage for this undertaking? If not me, who? If not now, when? The most important thing in life is not how much money you make or what kind of car you drive. It is what you can do to help others. Before the week was over, I finally found the courage to fill out the application and send it to VISTA Washington.

Two weeks before my availability date, a letter came in the mail that read:

> Dear Rose: May I congratulate you and express the pleasure I take in telling you now that you have been selected for training in VISTA. If you successfully complete VISTA training, you will be placed where your abilities and the needs of the poor are the greatest in order to maximize your contribution to the War on Poverty. Upon acceptance of the assignment, you will be registered in a VISTA training program scheduled to begin at nine o'clock in the morning on February 7, 1967, and conducted by the Northeastern Three training program in cooperation with the Northeastern University in Boston, Massachusetts.

The letter went on to give information concerning travel arrangements, finances and other personal matters, stating the training center will prepare me for work in rural settings in the Northeastern area of the United States, my work assignment preference.

When the letter arrived, I was working the afternoon shift at Munson Medical Center, arriving home at approximately eleven-thirty at night. When I saw the return address on that large envelope, my heart leaped for joy. I tore it open and began to read! I read and re-read every word until two o'clock in the morning and when I finally put it away and dropped into bed, I lay there awake for most of the remainder of the night!

How does a mother of three beloved, grown children, grandmother of a darling seventeen-month-old grandson, and daughter of the most wonderful, understanding mother in the whole world, feel about spending a whole year away from them in some corner of America she knows nothing about; a place where I was going to feel like a stranger in a strange land, where people would regard me as a "foreigner who has no business being here, we can take care of ourselves," where homesickness takes over and you don't know if you want to leave or if you want to stay; where the needs are so great you don't know where to begin? It was hard to leave. But, it was a matter of trying to live out a faith commitment that said not only is God real, but faith in God is the most important thing about living.

It was a cold, blustery Monday afternoon, a brisk, north wind sending big, fluffy snowflakes through the air as I made my way to the airport that February sixth, nineteen sixty-seven. With me were my mother, my two daughters, Judy and Nancy, and grandson Brian. My son, Tom, visited me the day before from his job in Kalamazoo, Michigan.

Several friends and co-workers were already waiting for me at the terminal. As we unloaded my luggage from the car . . . it struck me! Am I really leaving at last? Has the day finally arrived --- the day I've waited for these many months? Butterflies fluttered within me . . . my pulse picked up speed . . . a tear dropped! Mixed emotions began creeping up on me, but there was no turning back. My decision had been made. I was determined on becoming a VISTA Volunteer. "I am only one but I am one. I cannot do everything but I can do something. What I can do, I ought to do. And what I ought to do, by the Grace of God I *will* do."

CHAPTER II

UNEXPECTED EXPERIENCES

"I shall pass through this world but once. Any good, therefore, that I can do or any kindness that I can show to my fellowman; let me not defer nor neglect it . . . for I shall not pass this way again."

The plane trip to Boston was experience number one. It was my first plane ride and would begin a series of future experiences in my year with VISTA. Strangers who shared my plane seat soon became friends and helped to ease the anxiety I was feeling of what lay ahead.

The ride was a memorable one. City lights from forty thousand feet were beautiful after dark and the one hundred miles per hour tailwind allowed the flight to be a half-hour ahead of schedule.

Sitting in a triple plane seat assigned to me, between two strangers, I began to fear the unknown. I would arrive in a darkened and strange city. "How would I get to my hotel, assigned to me for the six-week VISTA training period? How would I register at the hotel? Who would be my roommate?" These and many other thoughts raced through my head and I didn't like them! Upon arriving, my fears were relieved when a cab driver approached me at plane side to ask where I was heading and if he could help. I explained I needed to get to Sherry Biltmore Hotel. He hesitated for a moment, then inquired, "Why have you chosen that hotel; there are others that may suit you better." I replied, "I must get to Sherry Biltmore as that is the one assigned to me during my six weeks in your city for VISTA training." He responded with shock and surprise, "Well, lady, if that's what you say and if that's what you want . . . I will take you there." He loaded my luggage into his cab and I was off to begin what would become one of the most adventurous, frustrating and happy years I have ever known.

Little did I know then, while riding in the yellow Checker cab, it would truly be an experience just living at Sherry Biltmore; a many-story hotel on Massachusetts Avenue, in the 'midst of Boston's Back Bay near the Charles River.

I checked in at the desk and gave the clerk my ID card and my reason for being there. I was told to go to a certain room on the third floor and there, waiting for me, would be the person who would tell me where my room is during my stay there. I arrived at the designated place and found the room empty. I waited what seemed like Eternity. There were several young people milling around by now; not really knowing where they should go or to whom they should speak. It was then I became one of them . . . a stranger in a strange city; in a hotel becoming a mystery to me already and fearing the unknown more than ever. Soon, from down the corridor came a young lady to ask if she could help me. I explained to her what the desk clerk directed me to do and that I was here to begin VISTA training. "Oh yes," she replied, "we have your room ready but you must first register your name and address." I was assigned a room on the third floor in which my roommate was already waiting; a pleasant sixtyish lady with a welcoming smile. After introducing myself, she spoke, "I'm Kate. I've been waiting for you and thought you'd never get here." A welcoming committee of one and just what I needed to hear!

Kate was from Pennsylvania and had relatives in Boston and knew the city 'somewhat.' While I unpacked, we talked about our families, life's experiences and looking forward to our 'year toward tomorrow;' when we would begin six weeks of making new friends, frustrations, wonderful instructors, walking twelve blocks three times daily to class and back in Boston's blizzards, intensive classroom instruction and having to learn all over again how it feels to be in a classroom with twenty-nine other trainees of different cultures and generations and to learn, too, that 'the ripples of a VISTA Volunteer CAN reach all shores.'

Our hotel room was large; with twin beds, two dressers, two chairs, an electric range and refrigerator but without a table. No problem. We spread a towel over the foot of one of the beds and made believe it was our table for meals. The closets were small but we didn't need much space as we were told in our travel instructions not to bring any more clothing than we absolutely needed; in the chance we may not be accepted into the VISTA program and would have to return home . . . a negative thought!

Bedtime brought other experiences. I would sleep in midnight darkness and the City was hidden from me. As I lay awake in my strange bed in a strange room, my first night in the big City, I thought of the many tall buildings in red brick, the weathered green copper and tall church spires; welcoming the lonely traveler. And what are those mysterious sounds?? Suddenly, in the middle of the night, Kate and I were awakened by earth-shattering screams! We sat straight up in our beds, breathless. "What was that? And where is it coming from?" We combined our thoughts and came to the conclusion: *at least our door is locked* and no one can reach us here. We tried to sleep but sleep wouldn't come as the screams continued.

Before long it was six o'clock in the morning and time we should be up and getting prepared to greet the day to which we both looked forward. A surprise came that first morning as I raised the window shade near my bed; a tall building stood right in front of me; or so it seemed, outside my window, so close, I felt I could touch it. It was the new fifty-two-story Prudential Tower just a block away. Stepping out our hotel room, we watched the snow blowing in through the broken window panes at the end of the corridor as we made our way to the elevator; strewn with litter and symbols of the night.

In the lobby our supervisor, Muriel, and other trainees were already waiting. We walked, blinded by blowing snow , across busy Massachusetts Avenue to a breakfast bar where we enjoyed the company of those with whom we would be spending the next six weeks.

Before leaving my home for VISTA training, I was a daily Communicant at Mass and learning of my assignment to Boston, I became concerned that a church may be many blocks from the hotel and I wouldn't have the opportunity to attend Mass before my classes. Much to my surprise, when I stepped outdoors the morning following my arrival, there stood my church, just two doors from the hotel: Ste. Cecelia, Patron Saint of musicians. I felt like singing God's praises and began to believe in miracles all over again!

Boston is one of America's oldest cities and New England's cosmopolitan heart, founded in sixteen thirty. Locals and veteran visitors recommend seeing the city on foot, especially the must-sees: Faneuil Hall, Harvard Square and Harvard Yard in Cambridge and countless museums and gallery-hopping on Newbury Street. The natives said, "We identify the seasons by the trees of Back Bay. In Spring, magnolias erupt into lotus-like blossoms of creamy white and deep pink. Come Summer, leaves fill in where lush flowers bloomed. In Autumn, the wind picks up, the sky turns moody and the elms of Commonwealth Avenue scatter their golden leaves. By December, the extraordinary structure of the American Elm is apparent on the mile-long pedestrian mall in the center of Commonwealth Avenue's wide boulevard, the geographic heart of Back Bay."

The old elms were bare of leaves in February, though stately, as they swayed with the breeze, appearing to call out to us . . . welcome to our city and our great Northeastern University, as we made our way through snow-drifted sidewalks to our first VISTA training class.

Walking was difficult as we tread our way to our classroom, six blocks away, past the Conservatory of Music building and skyscrapers of red brick.

VISTA training began at eight o'clock in the morning at Northeastern University on February seventh, nineteen sixty-seven. The program director, Dr. Melvin Howards, Assistant Professor of English at N.E.U., stood by as we filed into the classroom. The first order of the day was the requirement of pledging and signing the Oath of Allegiance to the United States of America. "I do solemnly swear that I will bear true faith and allegiance to the United States of America and will support and defend the Constitution and laws of the United States of America against all it's enemies foreign and domestic."

Dr. Howards explained the program and his expectations of the trainees. We were given daily schedules, lists of planned meetings, assignments for classes, schedules of field trips, introductions to various instructors and remedial reading literature, one of the major subjects during the entire six weeks, taught by Dr. Howards, assisted by two math instructors from N.E.U. Dr. Howards was a one-time school dropout himself. He is the founder of the nation's first dropout school located at N.E.U.'s campus and enrolled about two hundred fifty pupils at any given time, between the ages of sixteen and twenty-one. He also operated the only VISTA training center in New England at Northeastern U.

It was a real challenge attending classes with a group of young people fresh out of high school or college and retired men and women, and the need to learn how to study all over again and do homework! The trainees came from all walks of life and cultures across America. A retired couple heard about VISTA through their first Social Security check with the invitation to "Join VISTA and see the world." They responded. A lady of seventy-eight years young came from Florida and wanted to work with the young people after VISTA training. Another trainee from California, eighty-two, "didn't care where she would be placed, as long as it was in a warm climate." These two women from the Sunshine States had second thoughts, believe me, as they struggled through the blizzards of Boston on their way to classes.

Each training center had a full-time staff, headed by a director with supporting specialists, instructors and field supervisors, the focus being on one of the areas of poverty where the trainees would eventually be assigned, attempting to match the skills of the volunteer with the job at hand.

In the field experiences (the cornerstone of the training) we lived the lives of the poor in real settings. We learned firsthand about poverty's way of life and the needs and problems it presented, spending more than fifty percent of our training in actual poverty situations, e.g., homes of the underprivileged and slum housing developments. Our fieldwork was backed up with formal lectures, informal group discussions, workshops and personal conferences with staff members, on low-income lifestyles and related problems of the poor. We were instructed on the who, why, when, where and how of our training at hand, expected to attend meetings in the evenings after a full day in the classroom and drilled in conduct and behavior in hotel manners. Training consisted of twelve to fourteen hour days in a six day week plus Sundays whenever the staff called a conference. Evenings were usually filled with more classroom instruction and fieldwork.

The first three weeks of training was entirely classroom instruction in remedial reading and new math with speakers from government agencies, lectures and meetings, field trips, tests and exams and knocking on doors of slum housing complexes to listen to residents' housing complaints.

CHAPTER III

DO UNTO OTHERS

"You must have faith beyond faith . . . to the point you believe your faith will move a mountain."

The Poland Springs Womens' Job Corps Center in Maine was one of our field trips while in training, to get a firsthand look at their activities. This particular Job Corps camp was previously a playground for the rich; a retreat catering to presidents and the socially prominent. It was noted the world over for its waters, e.g., Poland Springs. The Graf Zeppelin once landed there to take on water for a flight around the world. Long ago the affluent abandoned Poland Springs for gayer areas. Now, the poor inherited the sprawling complex of buildings, designed to resemble a French Chateau. The rich came here to forget their jobs, now the poor came to try to get one.

Approximately eleven hundred young women, ages sixteen to twenty-one, were housed at Poland Springs in the Federal Government's largest Job Corps training center for women. Most of the girls were high school dropouts who didn't have a job and couldn't get one; they were there to learn vocational skills.

The Office of Economic Opportunity's announcement that the famous old resort would be converted into a young women's Job Corps Center caused considerable alarm amongst the local citizens who were announcing loud and clear, "How can this rural area absorb a sudden influx of eleven hundred young women?" One year after the Center began operating, the students were no longer a cause for alarm. Said a neighbor of the Center, "That place is just like a women's college, except for the subject matter." The girls signed out for trips to town and they had a curfew. Each weekend, young men from the nearby Naval Air Station traveled to Poland Springs for dates; each young man being carefully screened, even requiring that he bring along two references.

Kathy, age eighteen, couldn't wait to get back home to California. She confided, "Maine is too tame for me. . ." But she emphasized that she's content to remain until she masters the skills to become a florist. Flower arranging was among the courses offered including, clerical skills, veterinary training, bookkeeping, commercial arts, home management, culinary arts, among others. The average student stayed nine to twelve months with the average cost per student being five thousand dollars, including thirty dollars monthly salary and one hundred forty dollars for clothing allowance. The Center's operating costs totaled six and one-third million dollars for nineteen sixty-seven.

Job Corps are designed to offer needed help to a large number of young Americans who are out of school, out of work and out of hope. Its basic aim is to open a new future for thousands who do not complete high school nor qualify for a decent job and who cannot get these qualifications without getting out of the urban slums or rural hollows where they exist. The Job Corps offers job training and work experience courses in basic academic training, guidance and counseling. It does all this in urban training centers and rural camps throughout the country.

Many of the young people have never been away from home in their lives. Many have not completed eighth grade and read on a fourth grade level. VISTA's had a job to do at the Job Corps Centers. They taught classes in reading, math and typing, offered help in sewing, home management and whatever need came up where a VISTA could provide help.

Centers such as this still originate for thousands of young men and women who are dropouts or kickouts who cannot get a job; who, except for the Job Corps, would be doomed to the none-too-merry-go-round of the poverty circle. For many youngsters, it can be their first and last chance providing training for jobs and/or teaching them reading (remaining the one subject a must if one is to live in a world with (or without) poverty.)

When we visited the infirmary at Poland Springs (bustling with young women coming in with pinched fingers while working in the greenhouse, burned hands that accidentally touched a hot oven, sprains and a host of other scrapes and bruises received in their pursuit of learning new skills), it attracted me. And as nursing was my one love at the time, I confided to my supervisor upon our return: I would wish to be placed there as a VISTA Volunteer. She replied, "Rose, no you wouldn't, it is too confining for you. I know you would rather be in a more open environment." I was disappointed at her answer but accepted her reasoning. She possibly knew more about me than I knew myself!

Many volunteer government programs were in effect: VISTA, Day Care Centers for children, Adult Basic education, Head Start, Family Planning, Neighborhood Youth Corps, Foster Grand-Parents, Community Action Centers. The majority of these programs are still operating today assisting those less fortunate.

I found my cure for Winter lows in the skyline above Boston, when my roommate and I rode to the top of the fifty-two story Prudential Tower on a rare Sunday away from classes, just to enjoy the awesome view of skyscrapers, Fenway Park, Boston Harbor, and the numerous red brick edifices. From the observation deck, the frantic automobile and bus traffic below moved at a silent pace and snow and ice appeared as frosting on a cake.

The Prudential Insurance Co. of America, opening in the Spring of nineteen sixty-five, helped to generate the billion dollar building program with the fifty-two story Tower; the most striking feature of the new Boston skyline and the tallest building in Massachusetts at the time. Just below a top-floor restaurant, the view was stunning; a vast panorama of geography sprawled before us . . . the blue sweep of Massachusetts Bay; (iced over in February) the hump of two thousand six foot Wachusett Mountain rising beyond the rich farmlands to the West. The South shore curving towards distant Duxbury, enormous jets taking off from Logan Airport, the renowned Charles River and a million street lights twinkling and beckoning, was a sight to behold. And not to forget: the Great Atlantic in the distance. The three-and-one-half acre Prudential Center included a one-thousand-room hotel, two high-rise apartment buildings, several commercial buildings and a city-owned War Memorial Auditorium. The auditorium had the largest freight elevator in New England. I was astounded one day to see the doors open slowly and a truck-trailer rig drive out. The Pru was built on the Back Bay switchyard of the Boston-Albany Railroad, now running under it along with the Massachusetts Turnpike.

On another Sunday away from classes, a group of us decided to walk the Freedom Trail; crossing Boston Common to Old Granary Burying Ground, lying in mottled shade next to Park Street Church on Tremont Street. John Hancock is buried there, along with Peter Faneuil after whom Faneuil Hall is named; a combination public market and meeting place , a gift from him in seventeen forty-two.

Old Granary Burying Ground also claims the bodies of the parents of Benjamin Franklin, Mary Goose (regarded by many as the original Mother Goose) and the most famous of all, Paul Revere . . . "listen, my children, and you shall hear, of the midnight ride of Paul Revere." It seems appropriate that the oldest house still standing in Boston, a somber clapboard, belonged to Paul Revere. He left it on the night of April eighteenth, seventeen seventy-five, to warn the Minutemen of the approach of the British, who sought ammunition and arms stored in Concord. His house still preserves some relics of his life.

We traveled on our journey not far from the Revere house to Old North Church; in the belfry of which hung the lanterns signalling the departure of the British from Boston . . . "one if by land and two if by sea." Paul Revere left instructions with a trusted friend to hang lights in the steeple as he described the lantern-bearers long climb: "Up the trembling ladder, steep and tall, to the highest window in the wall." The midnight ride of Paul Revere has been immortalized in poetry. But the biographers described the dash as meaning no more to him than an exciting experience shared with William Dawes. (As I learned in my history book in grade school, Revere was a silversmith. But he also was a versatile craftsman who assisted the colonies in many ways. He manufactured gunpowder and cast cannon for the Army.) It is said, it was he who produced the State seal of Massachusetts.

The Freedom Trail traveled, our group visited Cambridge and Harvard, the country's oldest institution of learning and the foundation stone of the Bay State's prominent position in American education located in

Cambridge, Massachusetts. Today, it has become "University to the World."

The House of the Glass Flowers at Harvard Botanical Museum, where picture taking is forbidden due to the fragile nature of the flowers, is a favorite tourist attraction. Blown in delicate-colored glass by a famous artist, he then gave the entire collection to the University. Visitors can enjoy almost eight hundred fifty blown glass replicas of seven hundred eighty species of plants from morning glories to golden rods, with hundreds of flowering heads . . . some only one-tenth of an inch long . . . an experience to behold.

Walks in the Public Garden were enjoyable even in February and a not-to-be-forgotten trip to Filene's basement was a must. Natives told us, "When you visit Boston, a trip to see the Swan Boats on the Charles River and taking the subway to Filene's basement is a must-see." Not to forget is a tour to visit Old Ironsides, the famous ship Constitution, moored at Boston Naval Station in Charlestown Harbor.

The final three weeks of training took us to the slums of Roxbury, a suburb of Boston, to tutor black children with a low-grade reading level. My assignment was the ghetto area of Exodus, where black mothers fought to end segregation of schools, where fights broke out "because he looked at me the wrong way," where the kids refused to go to school "because I don't know how to read." "There's a whole City out there waiting for you, get out there and save the world," we were told by our project leaders. Another challenge had begun. By now, we were learned in remedial reading and, supposedly, ready to take upon ourselves the duty of teaching youngsters the art of reading.

I was assigned to Sidney, an eight-year-old, with a first grade reading level. He "wanted to be a fireman when he grows up." Whenever he heard a siren's screams, he left his seat in the middle of his lesson to run to the window to watch the fire trucks roll by, waving his arms in rapid succession. From the beginning, he was reluctant to let this stranger get near him, clinging to his mother as she encouraged him, but to no avail. Gradually, he warmed up to me, after giving him my undivided attention, courtesy and soft-spoken conversation. Soon, when he saw me coming through the doorway, he put on his best smile and headed for his usual seat at the end of the room. When I asked him if he was "ready for his lesson today," he began nodding in agreement.

Sidney was graded with every lesson, three times weekly. He began to show improvement ever so slowly. Then one day, to my amazement, he showed more interest in letters and words placed before him; to actually sound out the words when reading. I was happy that Sidney was finally able to show me that he, in fact, *could* learn. But I was sad also that it meant he would need to familiarize himself with another different person soon, as it was nearing the time for me to leave VISTA training. When our tutoring was near the final day, I brought along my camera to take Sidney's picture, with his mother's consent. She gave me her address "so I could write her" as she remarked,

"You have done so much for my little boy and I am so glad he had the opportunity to get some reading instructions, even for a short while, that I want to keep in touch with you." What a heartwarming message! Sad as I felt to leave him, after attempting to teach this little child of the ghetto, I considered it a privilege to be a part of his young life. Knowing the odds he faced of attending Harvard or Yale, nonetheless, I was now a part of his continuing education . . . and it made me very happy.

Exodus was in the heart of a crime area. It was the core of a riot the Summer following my placement as a VISTA, when a Friday night's battle broke out between the police and welfare demonstrators and their supporters. Whole buildings burned and many were seriously damaged including Exodus, the very building I taught Sidney.

Groups of trainees were also assigned to Columbia Point housing developments within the city. We knocked on doors of the apartment dwellers to hear their complaints of poor housing facilities, disrepair of appliances, walls, toilets, stairways, corridors plus busted-out windows where the snow blew in. The reluctance of landlords to do anything about it was unnerving to the residents and VISTA trainees alike. The trainees were attempting to come up with some real solutions for the tenants of the run-down apartments, even though it was like "trying to break through a brick wall." As one tenant remarked, "It's taken two months already and the landlord still hasn't come to fix the sink. My toilet ain't broke yet but I'm going to report it because by the time he gets here, it *will* be broke."

Field trips included a visit to the Brandon Rehabilitation Center in Vermont, housing children in all stages of disabilities. Cared for with help through the government-financed Foster Grandparent program, paid employees and volunteers, it was not difficult to see the change in personalities among the youngsters whenever a Grandparent showed up in their midst. The Grandparents were noticeably overjoyed at the sight of their little charges. A wonderful program bringing together the young and not-so-young and evident how much they needed each other. I believe in the old adage: When a rock is dropped in the center of a lake, eventually the ripples reach all shores.

Heavy snow was common in Boston in midwinter. When the weather turned into a blizzard and the snow swirled around the streets and highways and huge snowdrifts piled up and buses were delayed; we may have been riding those same buses and had a deadline to meet, getting back to our classroom for another evening class or meeting. Our rule was to be punctual for those get-togethers and when we realized the time was becoming short, we hopped off the bus and walked to our hotel room, sometimes two or three blocks, knee-deep in heavy wet snow. It was time saved we would not get otherwise, though we would rather have stayed in our warm hotel room. . . but we had to be about our VISTA ministrations.

Tommy Stevens, twenty-three months, and his sister Jenny, age four, lived in a ghetto housing complex where lead-based paint peeled and flaked from the walls. As a result of eating those lethal chips, both children developed increased appetites for non-food materials. Both were receiving intensive and painful treatments after tests showed high levels of lead in their bodies.

If it were not for the Office of Economic Opportunity's (O.E.O.) Legal Aid lawyers, Tommy and Jenny would have been just two more victims of this ghastly disease of slum housing, When the O.E.O. lawyers sued the landlord and launched an attack against the lead menace, causing brain damage and death among young children, the landlord was forced to repair their apartment where poison paint chips could be plucked like fruit from the walls. The suit was aimed at giving tenants the right to go to court to get the landlord to repair or remove a hazard to health and safety. The O.E.O.-funded Legal Aid Bureau also offered to assist private lawyers willing to accept lead poisoning cases. Lead poisoning is a serious problem in large and not-so-large cities. A biochemist who has written on the problem said it is probably the leading cause of death among children ages one to four who live in slum housing.

There are doctors who suspect that lead poisoning may be the key to the retardation and slow learning of many ghetto children. Diagnosis is usually made when the doctor is looking for it. The first symptoms, vomiting, constipation and abdominal pain, are so vague the child may not be taken to the doctor or he may think it is an intestinal disorder. The more advanced symptoms include convulsions, loss of consciousness, anemia, kidney damage and nervous system disorder.

Why should the lead menace be allowed to exist at all? If it were not solely a disease of the poor, living in poor housing, it may have caught the attention of more people. There was no law requiring the landlord to remove peeling paint and plaster and no law imposing penalties for permitting such conditions to exist. The lead poison problem demonstrated the fact that when housing was unsafe and unsanitary and hazardous, the tenant couldn't, in most cases, compel the landlord to make repairs and provide heat and water. Housing codes were not enforced in most cities, so while the landlord was free to break the law in most states, the tenant was required to live up to the letter of his lease or get thrown out. A Legal Aid Bureau, usually funded by O.E.O., made it possible to provide help for thousands of clients and singled out lead poisoning as a top priority item in its law reform program.

Training days, proving to be a very real experience and truly rewarding, were also very challenging. Counseling by a psychiatrist and personal evaluations were taking place regularly throughout the training period. There were tears and laughter, anxieties and frustrations, happiness and lots of camaraderie. VISTAs from other work sites of New England visited our classroom for a day relating some of their experiences in their assignments; possibly to give us an insight on what was in store for us in future assignments. An example was a group of four women VISTAs from a Maine project who told of being unable to find suitable housing upon their arrival. In their endeavors, they finally called on the local sheriff for assistance. He promptly offered them a room in the jail until appropriate housing could be found!

One afternoon, while riding the Boston Transit Authority bus on one of my many trips to Exodus for tutoring, sitting amongst the commuters, I suddenly realized I was the minority among them. My thoughts were of home and my family; my new grandchild about to enter the world and I cannot be there to welcome our new baby . . . a drop away from a tear! I found myself asking in self-pity, "Just what am I doing here?" As the bus rolled along through the slums, with its dilapidated buildings and deteriorating homes , shacks with children playing in the green, muddy water of the streets . . . all at once a sign appeared to me overhead on a highrise: GOD'S WORK MUST TRULY BE OUR OWN. I couldn't believe my eyes. I read it again. "Why had I not seen it before this? What was it telling me? At this time and at this moment? And the many times I traveled this path?" Before this time, I never felt as I did then: homesick and lonely . . . maybe burned out a little? As the bus traveled on, the sighting soon was history but . . . I could not get it out of my mind. It was as if those words were engraved in my thoughts, telling me something I could not grasp mentally just then. I soon realized I was given a message . . . a message to remind me, once again, what my choice in life was all about and why I chose to help the poor and underprivileged. I was here to learn how to help others less fortunate than myself. I needed that bit of encouragement at that homesick moment to keep going. A MIRACLE HAPPENED!

I knew that people who need people are the luckiest people in the world and I wanted to be that lucky person who helps people need each other. With a surge of unexplained energy, I sprang into my work with a vigor I could not comprehend. But now, I knew I must carry on if I am to do God's work here on Earth; and I knew His work must truly be my own! Since that occurrence, I've had some pretty exciting things happen but I can't think of a single one that held such enchantment as those seven little words on that highrise. While waiting for the bus to return me to my classroom following our tutoring session, I had the occasion to strike up a conversation with a potential fellow traveler. As we talked, I took hold of the lapel on my jacket holding my VISTA pin and proudly announced, "I'm a VISTA." The traveler looked blank, then turned the lapel on her own jacket and responded, "I'm a diabetic."

All of us realized that our extensive training could very well have caused some of us to throw up our hands and call it quits! But when a trainee became emotionally distraught, we began to appreciate our God-given privilege of being here. It happened a few days before we were to leave for our VISTA assignments. I was asked by our supervisor to stay with her in her room instead of attending classes for the day; just to make sure she would not be left alone or worse . . . escape. She became extremely restless to the point of becoming combative. I phoned for immediate help for a trip to the Emergency Department of a nearby hospital and accompanied her. Medication was prescribed and she was sent back to her room. Following classes for the day, I left her in the care of her roommates.

After causing much distress to her roommates, she recovered overnight, to the surprise of everyone. Even then, I was happy to have been given the privilege and opportunity of caring for this young lady who needed someone in times of difficulty. When it was any one of us who were in need, we had the help of those around us. The trainees themselves were a great source of encouragement to other trainees. They knew the feeling; they went through it themselves. In some instances, some of us may have considered our errors and problems as enormous, bringing us down to the nothing we already felt we were. . . then someone put out a hand, just far enough; someone looked at us as troubled persons rather than persons in trouble. This refreshing reflection from the lives of those who cared, somehow helped us to regain perspective, to trust once again and to carry on; if only for the reason we were there in the first place . . . to help people help themselves.

Returning to class the following morning, I was directed to Instructor Bill Thomas's office to receive my VISTA assignment. Anxiety took over as I was eagerly waiting to hear what had been chosen for me. When I was told, "Rose, you're going to Vermont to work with the University of Vermont Extension Service," I was not sure it was my preference. He noted my hesitation and said, "You don't have to accept this assignment. We can find you another." Just then, I felt a nudge and I heard, "You applied to help people in need; whatever or wherever that need may be." I replied, "Mr. Thomas, I will accept the assignment to Vermont." On my initial application to VISTA, I applied as a nurse but soon learned the need went far beyond that; a need I was not completely aware of at the time, until I arrived at my assignment site. When I accepted the Vermont assignment, it was then I realized ny VISTA training days were coming to an end and I would soon be added to the ranks of a true VISTA Volunteer serving the needs of the people of Vermont.

The last week of training was a difficult time for staff and trainees alike. New friendships had to be put on hold, if not terminated, a let-down on the part of the men and women who worked together for six weeks and now must part for different assignments. Fears cropped up: "How will the people I'm trying to help accept me? Can I really live in a poverty area? How can I survive without my newly-made friend?" The support and help the staff have given us would no longer be there. VISTAs needed the tenacity and dedication to carry them through. There were fears about being a real VISTA Volunteer, a new project sponsor, new living accommodations, people of a different culture with whom we were going to work. Problems had to be solved by ourselves instead of turning to the training center for help and support.

Having been a regular visitor and attendant at Holy Mass at the Carmelite Monastery near my home in Michigan, I made it my duty to visit the Monastery of the Discalced Carmelites in Roxbury, Mass., one of four contemplative houses for women religious in the Archdiocese of Boston. When I arrived at their door, following a block-long walk from the Boston Transit Authority bus, I introduced myself and explained my reason for being in Boston and bringing good wishes from the Sisters at Traverse City Carmel in Michigan. They welcomed me with open arms and invited me inside. Following an hour's visit, they took me on a tour of the monastery and its gardens. I felt blessed that I should have the privilege of being in their midst, especially at a time when I felt quite alone in the big city. They invited me to return for dinner when I had some free time and could get away from my many duties as a VISTA trainee. I returned, at their request, to "please do not walk off the bus alone. Let us know when you will be arriving and one of us will meet you." Located in the center of a crime area, the Sisters had a good reason for their request. Said the Sisters, "Our love is the church but the needs of the church are primary to any single rule. And if we can help, we should and do."

Graduation Day was a long-looked-forward-to affair. Edgar May, author of "Wasted Americans" and Pulitzer prize winner for his writings on welfare, was the principal speaker. We received a graduation certificate and VISTA ID pin in recognition of our VISTA training.

Once again, I pondered the thought I could not put into words, the reason for my decision of being a VISTA Volunteer, until I was exposed to the plight of the underprivileged during training. Only then did the true magnitude of the VISTA program begin to take shape for me. I have felt a real part of my Country. I have learned to live, eat and sleep in an unfamiliar environment. Even though I worked hard and became frustrated, I was personally and richly rewarded for my efforts. I had only a vague idea of what I would do on my new job as a VISTA ... only knew I was on my way to begin another new way of living. Life would go on and adjustments would be made. Tearful farewells were confided as we left our training center to begin new lives as VISTA Volunteers across America.

CHAPTER IV

I LIFT UP MINE EYES TO THE HILLS

Lift me, O God, above myself, that I may understand the needs of others in this challenging year ahead.

It was my birthday and the first day of Spring; a sunny, brisk March twentieth afternoon, when I left Boston's Logan Airport on a Yellowbird jet for Burlington, Vermont. All of beautiful Boston Harbor before me and the great Atlantic's beaming, sparkling waters reminding me of Henry David Thoreau, standing on a Cape Cod height when he said, "A man may stand there and put all of America behind him." But, there is another view . . . if he turns West standing on Massachusetts' main shore, "a man may stand there and put all of America before him." That's where my flight was taking me; to the beautiful, historic, New England State of Vermont.

As we flew away from the big city, Massachusetts' Mount Greylock began to take shape in the distance. Soon, a glimpse of Vermont's Green Mountains, Lake Champlain and New York's lofty Adirondacks came into view. "All I could see from where I stood was three long mountains and a wood. I turned and looked the other way, and saw three islands in a Bay." (author unknown)

Being my first flight in daylight, I was fascinated by the earth below; the mountains reaching up to greet me. I was eagerly awaiting my arrival, excited about entering another whole, new world and 'my year toward tomorrow.' As I entered the terminal lobby (not being told I would be met by anyone), I saw an attractive lady walking toward me with a smile. She spoke, "You must be Rose." I responded, "Yes, I am." She introduced herself as Polly Rowe, representing the University of Vermont Co-operative Extension Service in Burlington, the agency to which I was assigned. As we walked to her car, she explained that I, more than likely, would not be working in Burlington but in an area of Central Vermont. She would be driving me to Montpelier, Vermont's State Capitol, to meet my immediate supervisor, Edward Goodhouse, Windsor County agent for youth with offices in Woodstock, Vermont.

On the way, we talked about our life and work experiences and some of the needs I would encounter in my work with the underprivileged. She spoke of the need for a VISTA in the area of Bridgewater, a quaint village of eight hundred population, eight miles west of Woodstock. All the while, listening to her talk, my eyes kept turning to the friendly, beautiful Green Mountains and thanking God how fortunate I am to have accepted this assignment to New England.

Interstate eighty-nine, the superhighway on which we were now traveling, was just recently completed at a cost, in the late sixties, of a million dollars a mile; a huge sum in those economic times. It is a highway that winds its way through valleys, green rock-laden mountains: Mount Mansfield to the North, highest peak in Vermont; and Camel's Hump to the South. Crossing streams and the great Winooski River; a highway, sharing a part of its mountains in the form of rocks left standing in the median for the traveler to enjoy and marvel at. Rocks, whose colors are ever-changing in reds, blues, greens and the natural silver cast of shale and slate. On that sunny, March afternoon, they were covered with dripping icicles, glittering in the mid-afternoon sunshine, formed by the springs so abundant there; rock-covered cliffs reaching up to the low-hanging clouds with snowflakes fluttering past.

In Montpelier, I met Ed, who would be my support, my counselor, my friend . . . my supervisor, who would explain to me some of the needs of the community of Bridgewater, where I would be serving. On the drive with Ed to my assigned area, he spoke of a VISTA who had been assigned there for the past several months with whom I was to share a house trailer at Bridgewater Corners.

Darkness comes early in New England in Winter. And as he drove on I was unable to see the countryside and becoming more apprehensive about where he was taking me, with the feeling of being back in Boston's subways! He spoke of his anticipation of my working with the youth of Bridgewater's mountain region, stating, "Before this, nothing has ever been done in helping the young people learn a better way of life," and in what he hoped I would take an interest. He spoke of the poverty one encounters upon leaving the highway and driving the back roads; expressing a need for health education, employment assistance and remedial reading.

Before long, we arrived at the trailer I would call home, where I met Dorothy, my housemate, in her sixties, who had a degree in Home Economics. A General Services Administration auto was provided for our use in getting around the mountainous area of Central Vermont of which I was now a part. Dorothy drove me through the valleys and mountain roads where I became acquainted with some of the residents with whom I hoped to establish a rapport and become friends. My frustrations about where I could begin my journey overwhelmed me when I realized in what a large part of Windsor County I could expend my energy of finding the young people who were my main priority now.

General Services Administration, from whom we received the auto, has been maintaining it, notifying us whenever it was time to bring it in for a checkup in Burlington, usually every two months. When I took my road test from G.S.A., shortly after arriving at my VISTA site, I was given a car with a manual shift. I haven't driven one without an automatic for several years and have forgotten how to shift in reverse. OH! OH! "Will I pass my road test??" "Not to worry, " said my instructor, "we just don't happen to have an automatic on the lot for you to use today. Just make sure you don't <u>back out</u> of a Vermont driveway; that is illegal, due to the many sharp curves and limited distance viewing one encounters on the secondary roads."

A week into my VISTA service, homesickness took over, along with the anxiety of my desire to follow the hopes and expectations of my supervisors. Walks in the mountains along beautiful fast-flowing streams helped to ease my loneliness.

I began knocking on doors, introducing myself and explaining my purpose in their community. By home visiting, I had the opportunity to find a young man in his low-teens, the oldest of three children, with a low-grade reading level where I could now use my newly-acquired teaching skills. His father's main source of income was constructing snowshoes of deer hide. Skinned from a freshly-killed animal, he placed the whole skin near the wood-burning kitchen stove to dry. When he decided it was dry enough for weaving, he cut it into strips for the webbing, weaving it through, up and over, attaching it to the frame of the shoe, cut out of a special variety of wood. When finished, his snowshoes were a work of art. He was proficient also in making snowboards, used for downhill sliding, either standing or sitting. Using a special wood for the boards also, they measured approximately two feet wide by three feet long. It was just another way of trying to beat the pains of poverty, selling his work to locals and big-city folk who came to the skiing state to enjoy the Winter snows with their children.

Through a high school class visit, I discovered a group of teenagers interested in sewing and waitressing and volunteering. Midst my travels in finding the low-income, I constantly searched for a building in which to hold meetings, when and if needed. The board members of the Bridgewater Elementary School, through consultation with the principal, kindly offered me the use of a room in the school for evening get-togethers.

Business places were called upon for information on the needs of their community as were school officials, newspaper offices, the helping organizations (health and social service departments, Legal Aid), police departments, Extension office and many places who might offer assistance to help me find the ability to deal effectively with problems waiting to be solved.

Eventually, every home and business was called upon. School officials of Bridgewater and Woodstock were a necessary help in locating many of the young people from kindergarten through twelfth grade levels.

Driving along a scenic back road, I discovered a family with three sons, whose father had to let their hair grow "because he didn't have the equipment for haircuts." After much searching, an individual was found who offered to donate used hair clippers. I then found a barber to teach me how to cut hair so I, in turn, could teach the father. He was delighted, stating, "Now, I might even be able to take on other jobs of hair cutting in the neighborhood." And he did; being given the opportunity to put extra change in his pocket.

Even though I applied to VISTA as a nurse, I have learned the need went far beyond that. Nevertheless, shortly after my arrival, I discovered an elderly lady in the village in need of hands-on care following her dismissal from the hospital with a back problem. She lived with her disabled husband who was unable to care for her personal needs. A special effort was made to go to their home daily to assist with activities of daily living, making her my first priority for the day. I gave her morning care, assisted her out of bed, prepared breakfast for the two of them, straightened the house and counseled her husband, who had the responsibility of caring for her until I returned the following day. In time, she was qualified to receive help through helping organizations, working myself out of a job, as VISTAs were expected to do.

I was asked to speak to many local groups, telling and re-telling the workings of the VISTA program. As a result of meeting with a church-organized group of women from the Woodstock community, being impressed with the work a VISTA was expected to carry through a year of service, they offered monetary assistance for projects I had in mind for the young folk.

Children from the neighborhood visited me often to talk or to invite me to their home after school "because they had a surprise for me." I never refused. Sometimes, the surprise was a cookie and Jello with them on their back porches. Or it may have been a special surprise of soda pop and ice cream, after which we played games in the living room with the mother joining in. I enjoyed their friendship and felt privileged to have been invited to share a part of their young lives.

One Spring morning, eight-year-old Timmy from next door came dashing to my front door carrying a half-grown turtle, excitedly telling me how he rescued it from the center of the highway in front of my home. Following it along, crawling on his belly, as the turtle slowly made its way across my lawn heading for the road. He had to decide quickly what he was going to do with his new friend. I suggested, while praising him for his efforts, that he place it on the riverbank across the road where it would be safe. (?)

As VISTAs were given a library of books furnished by VISTA Washington for the use of the low-income adults and children, we were able to loan the books to whomever requested them. A bookcase was provided and set up in our home, enabling us to furnish them with reading material at their level of knowledge as long as the books were returned to allow others to borrow them. It was gratifying to see the many mothers and/or fathers accompanied by their children, choosing books carefully according to the level of their reading skills. The books were ninety-nine percent non-fiction stories on the home, animal habitats, plants, gardens and childrens' literature. Most mothers had knowledge of reading and being the main source of information when the child needed help with school work.

Our pink-colored trailer home was comfortably located next to busy Route Four, the main route between Rutland, Vermont, and White River Junction, Vermont, forty miles apart, connecting to One Hundred A South at Bridgewater Corners. The elderly lady who lived in the trailer prior to our arrival had a front yard with every imaginable flower planted there. We were told her flowers were all pink-colored as the trailer, her favorite color, where she spent her idle hours tending the flowers.

In the Spring after arriving, I noticed one morning the many tiny plants poking their heads above ground through the leaves and weeds. Much too pretty to neglect, Dorothy and I cared for them by hoeing and weeding. Not always a pleasant task, as I discovered one early morning as I was weeding before beginning my travels for the day; a spotted adder slithered his way through impenetrable weeds toward me. I stopped in my tracks to let him pass but he stopped too and raised his head as if to say, "This is my domain," or maybe it was his fearless way of welcoming me to his garden. Whenever I went outdoors to hang my laundry on the backyard clothesline, he was there to greet me. When I went out to my car on my way to keep an appointment, he was there. I wasn't sure just what his motive was, but at the same time I attempted to keep a safe distance between us.

It was a joy to discover that New England was home to the beautiful bluebird. I remember them clearly from my parents' farm as a child . . . the color of Lapis Lazuli, the semi-precious gem. In early Spring, when buds were breaking out on every living plant and tree, Dorothy and I took a stroll around the yard to look for signs of life. Lo and behold! a bluebird's nest tucked under the eaves of our trailer. "We must try to guard it from predators, " we told each other, "But how?" We'd quietly sneak a look around the corner of the house every day to catch some activity in the nest. Before too many days went by, we saw a nestful of tiny mouths waiting for that expected insect or crawly to pop in from their parents' beak. What a thrilling sight! New life. As the tiny birds grew, we'd see them fall from the nest one by one; a vulnerable time in their young lives. We hoped they would soon learn the purpose of their wings . . . before the stealthy feline found them.

In early May, the chimney swifts returned to Vermont. I remember learning about them in elementary school. In the Green Mountains and most of the Midwest and other remote areas, they nest in hollow trees. They are not colorful birds; almost entirely sooty-black, a large flock can appear as a huge tornado. You will never see them sitting on a wire as other birds; the only landing place is inside their nesting site. Their nests are made of small twigs, glued together with saliva. Chimney swifts are not necessarily chimney dwellers; they can be found in hollow trees that are dark and sheltered and barn silos. Insects are their food, caught on the wing as they twitter along through the skies, migrating birds who head back to their wintering grounds in South America.

Even though a television set was provided for our use in the trailer, the performance was usually nil despite an antenna in place on the six-hundred foot mountain behind our home. The news of the day was found in the *Rutland Herald*, a daily paper carried by the Bridgewater Grocery, two miles down the road. Local news came from a weekly paper, *The Vermont Standard*, published in Woodstock. A white clapboard house with four pillars adorning the front of the building served as the Bridgewater Corners Post Office. It was also the home of the Postmistress, situated next to a dirt road, carrying traffic behind our home to the old homes built there on the side of the mountain. Natives said, "Bridgewater marks the transition between rolling hills and steep mountains;" the area having the highest concentration of mountains in the State.

Across the road from our home, the Ottauquechee River flows beneath a one-hundred-year-old iron bridge, carrying Route One Hundred A South. A mountain looms across the road next to the foothills. The mountain was bare of leaves in March, being able to see the contour of the forest with its cedars, white birch and a variety of conifers and deciduous trees plus an occasional sighting of deer.

Mr. Mueller was an artist who lived with his dog a mile from our home. He enjoyed painting scenery and animals in oils. Some years ago, his dog had the misfortune of losing his hind legs in an auto accident, making it difficult to maneuver, dragging his small body along the floor or ground. Mr. Mueller, animal lover that he was, rigged up a two-by-three foot wooden-sided wagon with small wooden wheels attached to a leather harness that fit up and over the dog's back, under his belly and across the chest. Following many ambulatory adjustments, in time, he walked as if he had his own legs back. It was interesting to watch that little dog maneuver himself around with his little harness wagon taking the place of his hind legs. For auto trips, Mr. Mueller removed the harness and wagon, loading them into the car, then carrying the dog to sit beside him. They traveled together wherever the need took them.

His life was his dog and his paintings. He enjoyed recounting a day in midsummer when he decided to take a walk into the mountain behind my home with his sketch pad. As he made his way up the mountainside midst New England asters, goldenrod, milkweed and the thicket of the forest, he raised his head just in time to see a black bear standing on a large boulder, worn and rounded by the weather, not fifty feet in front of him. He grabbed his sketch pad and started sketching. The time was short and the bear had other plans than to stand there posing for his picture. He jumped off his perch on the rock in the direction of Mr. Mueller, causing him to make a quick getaway for safety, at the same time placing a mental picture in his mind of the beautiful animal soon to be in oils upon his canvas.

I had not heard this story before I made plans to take another trek up that same mountain one sunny, Sunday afternoon in July. With camera in hand, I started out. Soon, I was walking into junipers with their reluctant, spreading, prickly branches, stumbling over the brush that lay at my feet. Before long, the thicket became almost impossible to move through. I took a turn to get nearer the top. An open field came into view. There I saw eight foot tall seedlings showing a scar made by a gnawing animal, presumably a deer, attempting to reach a tasty bit of bark for his winter's snack. The scar being three-quarters of the way to the top of the tree, proving the depth of the snow in winter. In the mountains, where sugar house owners tapped maples for sap, I could see the height of the taps to be approximately five feet above ground, proving again that New Englanders can proudly say they truly have record-breaking snowfalls.

On my trek, I turned again to find a clearer view of the countryside below. Pictures taken, I wandered until I came to a very large slate-colored boulder, presumably five feet in diameter, that held a small, pure white rock. "That's funny," I said to myself, "why should a white rock be sitting square in the center of another rock in the middle of a mountain... unless someone put it there." I took a picture of it. The views were outstanding from the top. The sky on this sunny Sunday was a robin's egg blue, with fluffy white clouds floating across the sky, bumping into each other. Darker clouds were now appearing in the west that told me it just might be preparing to rain and I didn't have an umbrella nor a raincoat along; besides I wasn't about to get caught in a thunderstorm. It was time to head back home. Bear tracks were evident as were many small animal tracks. Black and red squirrels scolded as they scampered up and down the mountainside, darting into the thicket; while coons called to their mates. I wandered about a mile by now, it would take time to return; trudging through the junipers and thicket and Heaven forbid . . . come into contact with the bear whose tracks looked fresher than I cared to admit. My steps hastened as I hurried home while rain pelted down on me.

In a few days I received my developed pictures and, showing them to Mr. Mueller, he suddenly remarked, "Rose, that's the rock the bear was standing on when I first saw him. I put that white rock there to use as my landmark when I return again!" a co-incident. Another visit to Mr. Mueller's home brought more surprises when he showed me his painting of the bear he attempted to sketch before he had to scurry away from it's claws.

CHAPTER V

PEOPLE HELPING PEOPLE

"I can do all things in Him who strengthens me"

Only recently have observers begun to acknowledge that mountain people were forced into poverty; not by laziness or by geographical isolation, but by a history of being exploited by industrialists in years past, who bought land mineral rights for as little as fifty cents an acre, hired mountaineers at starvation wages to mine gold and then abandon the mines. There was exploitation by large lumber companies who purchased timber in the region at swindler's prices, removing the trees and leaving topsoil, essential for farming, to be washed away. Though many schools were available, it was not thought necessary to have an education; more important was the satisfaction of having money in their pocket to support families and making a living.

Working with young people couldn't be reduced to "rule-book form." Much was left to my own judgment. Respect was the keystone in working with youth. To even begin to think they will do whatever I hoped they would, I had to earn their respect and trust. I never made a promise I couldn't keep. I had to stay in contact with the parents *and* the young person. Rome wasn't built in a day nor is a child's life *rebuilt* in a day. This was a new experience and they didn't know how to accept it.

Maybe parents may have talked enough to their children but may not have listened enough; as a result, communication between child and parent could have been another of their problems. Taking the time to listen and understand what they were saying; helping them in their feelings for me and showing patience in their attempts at hands-on projects; it wasn't long before they began to respect me.

Nothing was ever done for the youngsters and they were not so sure they wanted to be doing anything different. I couldn't expect overnight miracles. When no one in the past took an interest in their young lives' activities, they had a hard time adjusting to so much attention all of a sudden. They rebelled and said, "Why is everybody doing so many things for us so suddenly?" To earn their rapport, they were given affection and attention; they have never known it and didn't know how to handle it. I had to "try to walk a mile in their shoes," being firm but kind, telling them what I expected from them in their projects and not judge if they made a mistake and genuinely caring for them whom I was trying to teach. And having rapport with them *before even beginning* was the key to forming a successful 4-H club.

Recruiting for 4-H was one of the more interesting experiences I have come across. There were no side-of-the-road mailboxes which didn't make it any less difficult to locate families with children. The mothers and/or fathers thought it was a wonderful idea to have their child in 4-H. From the beginning, I was providing the entire transportation; continuing to be an everlasting problem, the car always being somewhere else when it is needed the most. I was there to help people but I knew, too much help can harm instead of heal an adult. I wasn't there to help someone so much, I would become his/her crutch or shoulder. The transportation problem would be solved later; my priority now was to get these youngsters together to form a true 4-H club with proper applications and signatures.

There was such enthusiasm amongst the children and their parents; projects had to be chosen and materials provided before we could even begin. As VISTAs, we received zero funding, being our responsibility to secure a funding source. As a result, we held bake sales, rummage sales with clothing and many household articles donated by parents, neighbors and myself. I procured a meeting room in the Bridgewater Elementary School where we met weekly to hold our get-togethers, so necessary in order to inform the parents of our activities.

The first meeting of the Deer Run 4-H Club of Bridgewater (the name was chosen by vote amongst the young people) was held in the Bridgewater School and brought together the youngsters, parents and my supervisor,

Ed Goodhouse, who welcomed the group and explained the program. Forty boys and girls, ages ten to fourteen, were registered for the first-ever 4-H Club in the Bridgewater area. The boys chose woodworking and foods for their projects. The girls chose clothing, foods and crafts for their projects.

I was fortunate to find a grandmotherly-type lady who volunteered to teach sewing. She had grown children and "wanted to do something with her time." With her girls, she arranged for them to begin work on a dish towel and potholders. They used leftover terrycloth for the towels and colorful cotton for the holders. They then stuffed the holders with old nylon hose and stitched the four sides together for support. The girls were shown the workings of a sewing machine and allowed to try their expertise on a dish towel. It was an exciting experience until they were required to rip out their mistakes!

A 4-H mother asked to work with the foods group; as she remarked one day, "My girls like this group because they get to eat whatever we make when we're finished!" Trying out new recipes was an activity they enjoyed most.

A gentleman in his sixties, a carpenter by trade, volunteered to take the woodworking project and I worked with the crafts group. Some materials were provided free of charge for the leader and his boys by a lumber mill in Woodstock and the leader himself, as he stated, "I have so many scraps of wood that should be used up." The sewing leader said, "My children are gone from home now so I don't have anyone to sew for anymore and I need to use up the material I have left over."

All projects were hands-on activities and it gave the youth a great feeling of satisfaction when they could see the progress they were making. Our crafts girls began with paper crafts, given to their Moms and/or Dads for various occasions. They got a thrill out of a plaque we put together by cutting out pieces of black art paper in shapes of a frypan. We then cut shapes in colors to resemble two fried eggs and two strips of bacon, placing them in the center of the frypan, supporting the back with a piece of cardboard to hang on the wall with glued-on paper clips. The girls and boys liked the idea of being part of a group especially if their friend was a 4-H'er too. The woodworking leader and his boys cut out pieces of plywood for our craft project; used to make small trays with nails hammered around the perimeter about an inch high from which we strung yarn (a different color for each tray), varnished the bases and a cracker or utility tray came into being. They were presented to each girl's parent(s) with pride because now, they knew, it was an accomplishment they made themselves.

The lack of resources to carry out projects was a major problem with many low-income disadvantaged youth. Therefore, projects that required a minimum of resources have been designed and chosen. The 4-H projects of foods, sewing, wood and crafts were simple enough so they could carry them to completion, developing within themselves self-confidence and providing new experiences for which they could get a feeling of achievement. Flexibility in the projects had to be shown if one was to start within the knowledge, understanding and skills of the young person.

An important area in this phase of work was holding their attention and interest over an extended period of time. They wanted to make or build something they could see and show to others, especially their parents and school friends. The most successful approach was to plan several visits with the family to establish rapport before expecting them to assume responsibility. They became more receptive to my ideas of working on their projects when I showed them I cared.

Do I hear someone asking, "What is a 4-H club?" 4-H is a program for young people *and adults*. A program sponsored by a University or College. Programs for development, involving volunteers in providing positive, experiential and educational opportunities for and with youth. Adults are involved by giving of themselves as volunteers for creating programs the young people choose, supported by a caring adult.

The mission of 4-H is to create strong, healthy youth who are living in a complex and changing world. Programs are developed with support from several university departments, as well as other land-grant and higher education institutions.

Youth need to belong. They want to be a part of a club or a group . . . with a well-defined purpose and program, meeting their desires and interests. Every boy and girl needs to feel accepted. They need to feel successful, they need recognition and affection, they want responsibility. If 4-H members gain approval, independence, friendship, status, *belonging*, achievement and security, they will have a happy, well-balanced and successful life. 4-H has something special to offer when it comes to positive youth development programs. Many people don't realize just how important 4-H can be for a child. It is said kids who participate in 4-H get better grades than kids who are not in youth groups. 4-H'ers learn life skills, such as decision-making and cooperation, helping them become productive adults.

4-H has a long tradition of working with young people. The kids learn about the importance of helping others in whatever way they can all their lives. 4-H members are not forced into a project; they are assisted in their decisions by their parents and the volunteers who work with them. It gives them an opportunity to learn things relevant to their lives, regardless of where they live or go to school. Adults are an important influence on kids, permitting them to work together and benefit from each other's lives.

The 4-H pledge is recited before every meeting of the group:

I pledge my head to clearer thinking

My heart to greater loyalty

My hands to larger service

My health to better living

For my club, my community and my Country.

4-H's primary goal is to provide opportunities for all young people, ages five to nineteen, regardless of where they live, their socio-economic background or the size of their city or town. There are no state or national dues. The cost to 4-H members *solely* depends on the choices made by them, with support from the leaders of the Club and their parents. 4-H programs are supported on Federal, state and county levels. Through a Co-operative Extension Service, the program is committed to helping people put information to work in their communities, for their families and for themselves.

May Day falls on May first and traditionally it is celebrated by dancing; adults and children alike, around a Maypole with each dancer holding a long brightly-colored ribbon attached to the top of the Maypole. Crowning of a May Queen or a religious celebration may be held in area churches, by the crowning of Queen of the May, the Blessed Mother of God. Festivals are held for a more traditional celebration throughout America.

For the 4-H group's May Day celebration, our whole group put together fresh flowers, donated by local florists, placing them into colorful baskets made of craft paper and tied with assorted colored ribbons. As we walked to the homes of the ill and elderly, those young people spoke of their interest of actually having the privilege and opportunity of "giving some little thing to these people who needed it most." We placed the baskets on the doorknobs and left. In the cases of the disabled and elderly with whom we were familiar, we knocked first and let ourselves in. What a warm feeling it has given the recipients who couldn't believe that someone cared enough to bring a gift because "we didn't think anybody would remember us!"

A juniper is described as a small evergreen shrub or tree of the pine family, with scale-like foliage and berry-like cones. It is an innocent description of the plant but it doesn't tell us anything about the roots; one of my learning experiences when a steep embankment near my trailer home required some conservation work to protect it from erosion. It was then I decided junipers would be just the answer to fill in the hill. The bank has been eroding for many years already and it would be a good project for the young people of the newly-formed 4-H club.

As I drove around the countryside attempting to locate a field where junipers grew, I saw a farmer standing in a field where many sizes of the plant were growing. I stopped my car along the roadside as he started walking toward me. I introduced myself and inquired if he knew who owned the land so I might ask permission to remove a few of the shrubs for a 4-H project. The farmer answered, "I own this piece of property, just come and take all you want, they're not doing me any good."

There were plants as small as a half-bushel and as large as five feet tall; spreading their branches every which way. I made arrangements with him to pick up several in a few days. He called out to me as I was about to drive away, "Come get all you want. Come anytime." I was grateful for that offer; I thanked him and was on my way. Little did I realize then, he may have been laughing all the way home!

I returned in a couple of days with a group of strong-armed 4-H'ers and two shovels. We approached the area with great anticipation as now the bank will have plants to protect it from the rush of water; washing it free of sand and gravel. "Let's try this small one first," I told them. A shovel dug below a smaller juniper. UGH! It wouldn't budge. "Let's try this one." The shovel was again thrust under another smaller plant and that one was not about to move either. We didn't give up . . . one after another, every thrust of the shovel was like digging into solid rock.

I could feel the eyes of the farmer upon us as we struggled with the reluctant plants, probably chuckling to himself all the while. In due time, we gave up on digging, trying to decide whether that was such a good idea after all.

On our way back home, we gave it a lot of thought, the 4-H'ers trying to come up with other methods of removing the junipers until we ran out of ideas but I was determined to save my embankment from being washed away completely.

Again, I traveled the back roads searching for a plant suitable for planting, finding just what I knew would be the answer to my dilemma; a beautiful row of young white pine seedlings alongside a back road. Were they on private property? Or were they on road right-of-way, a legal distance for digging? I contacted the Vermont State Highway Department for information. I was told, "If a plant is x-number of feet from the center of the road, whether highway or back road, it is legal to dig. Bring along a yardstick and if it shows legal limits, you can take the pines." It did! HAPPY DAY! Once again, I gathered a 4-H leader, three young men with shovels, and we headed back to get the beautiful little pines. We dug ten ten-inch seedlings, planting them carefully on our bank.

As it was a hot, dry summer, I carried twelve-quart pails of water daily from my home next door, to save the plants from drought. They all thrived for several weeks until four of them began to show signs of distress. We nursed them to no avail. The remaining six grew to healthy white pines. Now, twenty-eight years later, they have grown to fifteen feet and still growing, shading the bank from the sun and preventing the washouts that plagued it for so many years.

As the bank needed color too, a 4-H leader and I planted pink phlox around the perimeter. Today, the flowers come up with a burst of color whenever May rolls around.

The hill where the pines are growing had a black-top walkway with an iron railing, used by the elderly who came down the hill to shop at the Corners grocery. The railing was badly in need of repair, rusted, with broken sections. Once again, I contacted the highway department for assistance with the problem. Two workers arrived to assess the condition of the project and materials required for repairs. In a week's time, a crew arrived to replace the entire railing, much to the benefit and enjoyment of the citizens of Bridgewater Corners.

Life of a VISTA Volunteer

I am a guidance counselor, readin', writin' and 'rithmetic teacher.

I am den mother, referee, newspaper editor, reporter and printer.

I am public-relation person, chauffeur and banker.

I am tailor, medic, friend, buddy and informer.

I am public enemy number one and greatest pal in the world.

I am satisfied, frustrated, happy, disgusted, depressed and ecstatic.

I want to stay and I want to leave.

I guess I'm just a typical VISTA.

From: *Ode of a VISTA Volunteer*
Anywhere, U.S.A.

CHAPTER VI

SO LONG AS WE LOVE WE SERVE

"You cannot do a kindness too soon, for you never know how soon it will be too late."

Volunteers committed themselves to a calendar year of full-time service following completion of training and assignment to a project. The commitment included living amongst and at the economic level of the people we would be serving, without regard to regular working hours. All VISTA Volunteers needed to have the desire to serve and persist through frustrations. The emotional and physical strength required for sensitive and difficult work, the ability to approach problems in terms of possible solutions and the capacity to give needed assistance, was the role of a VISTA who was the assistant, who tried to help people develop leadership abilities, rather than head community person. We wanted to fit into the social life of the community in which we served because we were attempting to become a part of that community . . . not to make changes but to help the people find an easier and better way of life.

Approximately four months into my VISTA service, I was invited to a reunion of the VISTA trainees for a day. I hopped on a plane at Lebanon, N.H., for Boston; a welcome change of pace as I was already busily involved in projects and there were times when the days seemed to be lacking many hours in which to finish my work for the day. A Rest and Relaxation time sounded like a good idea, if only for a day.

It was good to see my former classmates again, re-hashing our training days at N.E.U. and re-kindling friendships. Interesting, too, to hear others' similar frustrations. At times, I felt I was the only one with problems; trying to encourage people to respond when I knew they could or should

At the reunion, I met a young VISTA who was assigned to the Passamaquoddy Indian Reservation in Maine. He spoke warmly of his work in what he had already been involved for several months. I explained to him of my interest in serving on an Indian Reservation, but my training at N.E.U. didn't prepare me for it. He then asked if I would like to visit him sometime that summer to get a glimpse of the activities on a Reservation. Expressing my appreciation for his invitation, I considered it a privilege to have the opportunity to visit there. He then requested that I not arrive alone without notice . . . that he preferred to meet me at the entrance gate himself. I looked forward to the visit but as it turned out, I was unable to get away from my many projects and having the privilege of driving a General Services Administration auto for transportation,

I was required to place restrictions on certain areas where the government vehicle was allowed to be driven or even parked. To abuse my privileges would have cancelled out my appreciation for having the use of an auto.

By now, the Bridgewater Deer Run 4-H Club was in full swing and prospering. Much interest was being shown by the youngsters and their parents. Materials were being donated for projects by various organizations. The craft group grew to two separate units and soon another woodworking group would be starting with five boys enrolled. Other young people were hearing about the fun and hands-on projects the original group was enjoying and wanted to belong. One craft unit began learning embroidery and constructing litter bags out of brown paper sacks. Wall plaques were being introduced and several more difficult crafts the girls wanted to try.

The woodworking class was learning how to use an electric drill under the competent management of their leader, Mr. Snow. They learned how to stain wood and build a footstool and bookcase.

My home was busy with many visitors. They came with information regarding their home life, some to volunteer their services (that, to me, was the most desirable of all and it showed me they cared). Many came to invite me over for pie and tea. Families came to ask if I would accompany them to a dance Saturday night. Some came to bring their sewing and talk. Others wanted me to know of a certain case of child or spouse abuse. I followed up with each and every one of their requests and concerns, at which time the helping services came into play. Dorothy and I had invitations to accompany Herb on fishing trips to Silver Lake at Barnard. He supplied the fishing poles and bait and we supplied the transportation and a picnic lunch. What fun to cast a line out from shore and suddenly feel a hit on the line!

As I sat at shore's edge on a wet chunk of sod, barefoot, dangling my feet in the water, I unexpectedly felt a slight nudge on the back of my heel. Was it imagination? Was it the action of the waves washing against the shore? I felt it again and again. It puzzled me. What could it be? Stepping into the water, I checked under the overhanging sod and found nothing. Returning to my position on the wet sod, I felt it again. Lo and behold, it was a ten-inch rainbow trout, nudging at my heel with its mouth, as I watched, bent over to get a better look. What was his motive? I never did find out. Probably trying to tell me it was *his* abode and was not about to let me in. Nevertheless, it was another of life's experiences.

I felt now, I was happily becoming a part of the community where I was assigned and knew I have successfully established a rapport with the residents.

Through the cooperation of the University of Vermont Extension Service specialists and consultation with various departments of the local Co-operative Extension Service, I began recruiting for a waitress/waiter training course. I soon had several young women interested in becoming waitresses, as they requested soon after my arrival in Bridgewater.

Several local eating places volunteered their expertise through employees and the owners themselves, to present a class on various aspects of waitressing.

The course included job applications, pleasing and serving the customer, job skills, culinary arts, personal grooming and sanitation, participation and demonstrations by the students and responsibility of the employer and employee. The class had the privilege of having the talents of Nutrition Specialists as volunteer instructors from the University of Vermont Extension Service in Burlington. The six-week course was held in the Bridgewater Elementary School without cost, with six young women enrolled. It was followed by presentation of certificates, donated free of charge, by the Elm Tree Press of Woodstock. As a part of the training, plans were made for taking the young women to dinner at the close of the course, to a Woodstock restaurant. Kathy Wendling, restaurateur of Woodstock, graciously offered the use of her establishment for the group. I did not have the slightest idea where the money would come from to pay for our dinner, presumably from my own pocket! In contact with several local people, a gentleman donated a sizeable sum for our meal. He stated, "I want to do something nice for the young people of our community." A course evaluation was completed by the group with many positive comments.

Soon thereafter, three young women and two 4-H Junior Assistant Leaders began volunteering at a Woodstock Nursing Home, naming their group Geri-Teens. They began with once weekly visits, extending to twice weekly after three weeks. The residents enjoyed the young folks and expressing their feelings said, "It was the best thing that ever happened to us." The girls, in turn, had the good feeling of the privilege of doing something constructive and worthwhile. As some of the residents were housed on the second floor, the meals were also served there. It gave the volunteers the opportunity to assist the regular employees of carrying the food trays up the flight of stairs, not a menial task.

The girls read to the residents, wrote letters, took them for walks in the garden area and visited with them; what may have been the one most important duty of the day. The experience was satisfying when the girls realized how much the old folks needed them and how it could become a future paying job. I worked with them for less than a month, after which they found other transportation; my job then was to offer counsel and support.

By now, everyone knew "Rose is the lady we call upon when we need help." I was receiving calls in the middle of the night. They knew, now, of services available: Legal Aid, Social Services, Health Department. Many instances came up when I would phone for assistance from these helping organizations.

A home I visited frequently became a source of great concern when a member of the area made me aware of the fact that something was dangerously out of line at the home. I visited the family to check it out and discovered the mother was home alone with the three small children. When I made the comment to her that they were alone, she confided to me, "Oh, he left for parts unknown." She then stated one of the little boys had been sat on a hot wood stove by her husband, "Because the child refused to go to bed." As the mother explained it, "I wanted to take Johnny to the doctor but had no way to get there and no phone to call for help. Besides, my husband didn't think it was necessary or important and refused to take us." She stated, "I finally got a neighbor to take us to Emergency. I didn't want the doctor to know why his seat was so red and blistered until the doctor asked Johnny how he got the burn and he told the doctor his daddy sat him on the hot stove."

As a neighbor confided in me, "I told the mother something had to be done for the child," who then took mother and child to the Emergency Room one week later. His third degree burns became infected, requiring several return visits to the doctor with assistance of Social Services. The father didn't escape from the incident lightly. Through consultation with Legal Aid, he was found and arrested and sent to prison for an extended period.

Health care was much in demand. Pregnant women needing assistance at times of home delivery, children and families becoming ill, couples' marital problems, divorces in progress. The helping organizations were a necessary help for so many. The Lion's Club were helpful in furnishing eye glasses for the needy children and adults. 4-H camping was about to begin and recruiting was a real challenge; a difficult task encouraging parents to allow their child the experience of camping and being with other young people their own age. Then the happiness the children exhibited when told by the parent, "Yes, you can attend camp," was all worth the effort for me.

Ricky, a young man of twelve years with a second grade reading level, was enrolled in my remedial reading class. He seemed happy when he was told by his parents he could attend camp, "Just to stop your begging." Clothing was secured for him for the week through a helping organization, application processed and the day arrived for him to leave for camp. I furnished the transportation and Ricky and his mother and I were on our way to the "great adventure," forty miles away. As we registered him, he took off running around the grounds, trying out all the play equipment and swings; happy and excited about his newly-found experience-to-be(?). As his mother and I returned to the car to begin unpacking, Ricky suddenly appeared and announced to us, "I'm not staying." No amount of coaxing by his mother and staff made any difference. He ran back to the car, positioned himself inside and refused to come out! More frustrations. Ricky and his mother were transported back to their home and now it was my problem once again to find another camper to take his place as long as the entrance fee was already paid and nonreturnable.

Sylvia was eleven, a young lady whose mother died some years ago and her father, being very protective of her, was apprehensive about allowing his daughter the privilege of attending 4-H camp for a week. With encouragement and assurance, he finally agreed that "it may do her some good to be with other young people" . . . all these plans being made on his back steps.

Again, clothing for a girl for a week had to be found, new application processed, and Sylvia was transported to camp. Her father didn't allow her to leave alone with me; he recruited his married daughter and her husband to go along. I suggested he accompany us to view the camp surroundings where his daughter will be spending the week; he refused. Being the sole provider for his family and caregiver, he chose to remain at home with his two older children.

Even though the underprivileged protected and guarded their children, they chose to live as their parents and grandparents lived and in so doing made their labors slow and difficult. Money was rarer than leisure. Most mountain people learned to live in a "make do or do without" environment. Securing an adequate supply of food was a primary concern. Some raised vegetable gardens planted along the sides of the house and contained everything usually found in a garden: beets, radishes, corn, lettuce, tomatoes, turnips, cucumbers, sometimes a horseradish root was growing along one side of the plot. Some would not bother with a garden or didn't have the money to buy seed.

At the time of my VISTA service, food stamps were unheard of. The government food surplus was something they looked forward to receiving every month, even though it has never been intended to provide a complete diet. The surplus *did* supplement the foods purchased by the low-income. It was difficult for even a skilled cook to prepare from fifteen commodities. Peanut butter was one of the foods given but even though it is a highly nutritious food, there is only so much one can do with it. One example of how it could be used was with a peanut butter stew as follows:

PEANUT BUTTER STEW

3 cups peanut butter
1 cup tomato paste
2 tsp. red pepper
4 tomatoes
2 tsp. salt
4 chopped onions
2-4 cups water
Cooking oil
2 lbs. stewing meat

Squeeze peanut butter and 3 cups water through fingers into a large pot until thoroughly mixed. Add tomato paste. Place over med. high heat and stir until well mixed. Saute onions and chopped tomatoes. Add onion and tomatoes to peanut butter mixture in large pot. Place over med. heat and stir until of consistency that will run through the holes of a large strainer spoon. Add salt and red pepper to taste and return for another forty minutes. Brown stewing meat in large pan. Add meat to peanut butter mixture and cook for one hour. If mixture becomes too thick, add more water. Serve over rice.

How's this for a gourmet meal?

Other recipes included refried beans, buckaroo beans, peanut butter yeast loaf, tuna casserole made with tuna, eggs, oatmeal and milk as in meat loaf. One of the commodities received was Bulgur. Very few cooks knew what it was used for, let alone knowing how to cook with it. Bulgur is simply whole-wheat kernels that have been soaked, cooked and dried. After some of the bran is removed from the dried wheat kernels, the remaining kernels are cracked into small pieces. It cooks quickly. Add one cup bulgur to two cups cold water. Bring to a boil. Cover, simmer twelve to fifteen minutes or until tender. It may be frozen at this point. Combined with oatmeal and dried fruit, it becomes a breakfast food. Or mix bulgur into ground meat for burgers. Many other dishes may be prepared with bulgur.

Windsor County Co-operative Extension Service provided recipes to be handed out to meal preparers to have some knowledge in preparation of foods with minimum instructions. It was just another service consumed by the VISTA Volunteer.

Some women had pride and didn't want anyone to know they didn't know how to cook, making it a challenge for VISTAs to offer help and/or suggestions. I learned to drink my coffee black. In my home visits, I was offered a cup of the caffeine-laced liquid only to find that most didn't offer milk because they had none to offer.

Some of the impressions of a minority of the natives toward the VISTA Volunteer was, "here she is, trying to change our lives and our way of doing things; maybe even taking our children away." A very real relationship and rapport had to be established before I could even begin to make any headway in what I was attempting to accomplish. I had to show compassion toward them and friendliness in our conversations. I had to let them know I wasn't there to change their ways of living, only to try to make it better. I had to let them know I cared for them by making frequent visits and not making promises I couldn't keep.

"I hope you don't have to wait much longer to start building," I stated to the disabled man who was receiving welfare. Through Community Action Council self-help programs, this gentleman was now on a waiting list to erect a new home. His present dwelling was a tenant farm shack. The self-help housing program would help him with finances and he in turn would have help from friends and/or relatives to build his home.

While the state existed in a pastoral setting for centuries, the transition to a more urban-oriented culture was taking place fifty years ago when the nation's economy was at its lowest point. It began with the abandonment of borderline-operated farms and the migration to the cities by the children of these farmers. Natives said, "Vermont had more cows than people at one time." And the farmers tending to these animals had a good living from it. The farmers were now parceling their holdings to ski areas and vacation resorts . . . a land boom they called it. But the prosperity had failed to filter down to the rural poor. The larger home owners selling or taking land out of production or diminishing their dairy herds, made the impact severely felt by farm workers and their families.

Some low-income people raised hogs, a milk cow, perhaps a few chickens. the main source of income locally was the Bridgewater Woolen Mill where usually both husband and wife worked. Woolen mills were prevalent in the Northeast until demand for wool could be better found in larger states. Children were forced to drop out of school as soon as they reached the magical age of sixteen to help support a household. Once these young people left school, it was next to impossible to get them to return to classes of any kind. When they finally found a job, it was usually low pay but it was enough to them . . . to have money in their pockets.

Problems such as these are not only found in New England; they are in terms of people all over the country. What happens is you get a people in deprived circumstances who don't have an educational background in order to obtain the kind of jobs available. VISTAs and other volunteers struggled to give assistance to the less privileged and tried to make a better life for them. New methods of teaching math and reading were introduced and accomplished and challenges met on the road to the elimination of poverty by showing the poor how they can help to help themselves.

In all my visits to homes of families during training, I have never seen any of them with toys . . . children ages five to twelve. When they played away from the house, it could be near the river running along the front of their homes next to the dirt road. Or it could be in the neighbor's yard. When they tired of it, back to the house they'd go or near the river bank where the water runs deep, especially in Spring or late Winter. They again returned to their yards with other children, rested a bit and started the whole ritual all over again. The girls never had dolls, instead, they found a small patch of dirt and with spoons dug up the dirt into dirty paper plates. I asked them what they were playing. "Nothing," was the reply. Many poor parents could not provide any of the extra attention or the pennies kids like to carry in their pockets or toys the children need. Life was idle play most of the time; no chores to keep little minds busy, no waste baskets to empty, no running to the store.

Help wasn't needed to prepare dinner because there were never any plans in preparing it. Food was scarce until the arrival of the next batch of surplus food. Occasionally, mothers seemed to withhold affection from their children, not because they rejected them but they wanted to train them away from dependency on them. It was not unusual to see eight or nine-month old babies pulling themselves up and down a flight of stairs without help. Or a three-year-old girl preparing her infant sister's milk and changing her diaper. Many poor children are taught to care for themselves in the rough and tumble play of the streets and playgrounds.

CHAPTER VII

"... A MAN'S REACH SHOULD EXCEED HIS GRASP"

"No man is an island, entire of itself; every man is a piece of the continent; a part of the main..."

As the months rolled on into Fall, I was beginning to feel really at home in my Country surroundings. Autumn in Vermont, as in most of New England, is all pretty reds and yellows and oranges and bronze, as its foliage readies for the long Winter. Vermont, in tourists' eyes in any season, is an endlessly unfolding packet of "wish you were here" postcards. So pretty, one cannot believe it! You want to stop your car and take pictures, study woodlands, marvel at hamlets nestled in the valleys of green mountains, white church spires, covered bridges, countless bake shops and antique shops galore. Even rocks in New England have a special brightness... purply pinks and greeny grays dotting the expressways like jewels spilled from a giant necklace. And the ever-changing colors of the mountains. Beautiful, picturesque, historic, maple-syrupy Vermont and when you turn off the highways... where the most beautiful scenery can be found along the backroads, where the poverty of the state rears its ugly head . . . until I stumbled onto certain backroads . . . until I was led by my instinct as a VISTA into an area that contradicted the beauty of New England all at once; the invisible poverty was there before my eyes. And no matter that people in ghettos have troubles and Reservation Native Americans have troubles and the South's migrant workers have troubles; here in this rugged land of our Founders, the troubles of poverty have raged in isolated anguish for a much longer time than we dare to admit . . . this, after all, is where much of what we are was formed.

The hidden poverty showed as the little girl waited for dinner in an old farm house without glass in the windows; she, her two sisters, baby brother and parents subsisted on welfare allotments as generations before them have done.

During training, many families with whom I visited often apologized for the deteriorating condition of their homes. If they did not make improvements, their property taxes were not imposed upon them and many did not pay taxes for that reason. Shacks stood empty in the middle of a neighborhood, windows knocked out, a haven for rats, a playhouse for neighborhood children. Houses, once sheltering families, have been pronounced "unfit for human habitation" and slated for demolition.

Interspersed among them were similar houses with curtains still at the windows and still inhabited. Welfare mothers paid twenty dollars a week to live in a few of the rooms; because they couldn't find anything else. There was a critical shortage of low-rent housing and what was available went to the middle-income person with a good credit rating and a small family. The poorer head of household was not in a position to demand any particular standards for his money. If the tenant complained, the landlord needed only to give him a thirty-day eviction notice.

Large numbers of the poor could only dream about planning for other things. Some of the homes were the roughest looking houses I have ever seen. I turned my car onto another dirt road and saw shacks with rusty tin roofs, shanties with barnboard siding cracked from the weather; places built haphazardly with cast-off lumber. I turned onto another trail . . . muddy with white birch tree branches fallen across it. I got out of my car and attempted to remove them; taking some will power and not just a little arm power to get them out of the way far enough to allow me to pass. I parked my car alongside a tiny green-roofed shack, abandoned and barely standing, twisting in different directions as if it couldn't decide which way to fall. The front porch collapsed at one end, the brick chimney tilted, the windows popped their eyes.

The neighborhood floods after a heavy rain and the end of the road was a rain-made lake. The front door was barely hanging by its rusty hinges and holes in the roof cast specks of light upon the naked windows. I walked in. I could see no one lived here for a long time. A fragment of ratty carpet covered a piece of the floor and paneling was falling off the walls exposing their newspaper insulation innards.

Bees and wasps were everywhere, doors fallen backward; the whole place had the humid smell of rotting wood. At one of the many other shanty houses nearby, children were laughing, running, playing in a dirt yard; a stagnant canal of green cloudy water reeked at their feet. They stopped and stood when I introduced myself, staring at the ground, kicking the dirt for a long moment. Then one of them spoke, "No one is living in that there house anymore." I inquired, "Do you have friends around here?" A boy answered, "Baseball friends." I asked, "Do you visit them?" He replied, "Sometimes." "Ever invite them to your house?" I inquired again. The first boy answered, "Oh, sometimes I do, but they maybe won't like our neighborhood, the way we live." I asked, "What way is that?" He replied, "Tin houses, holes in the roof; stuff like that." I inquired again, "Is it that they would not like the way you live, or do you not want them to *see* the way you live?" A long pause, then the second boy spoke, "We don't want them to *see* the way we live." "It's embarrassing to you?" "Yeah." "Do the kids on the other road live this way? I asked. "No, brick houses, sidewalks." "What do you think when you visit them?" I asked again. He hesitated a long time, then asked a question, "Why couldn't *we* live in houses like that?" "And why can't you?" I asked. He responded quickly, "Our parents don't have the right education." "How are you doing in school?" I asked again. "Straight A work." "What do you want to be?" I inquired. "An architect," he answered. "And where do you want to go to college?" I inquired again. He spoke quickly, "Harvard or Yale." His answer caught me off guard. I was glad for his ambition but sad at the long odds he faced. It was time for me to take leave and call on other homes. As I departed, I called to the youngsters, "I wish you all the best." Sincerely spoken words; if only I could take all of these children and fulfill their dreams of Harvard or Yale.

I hoped for a picture of these youngsters in their surroundings. But VISTAs could not expect to go into a neighborhood and start taking pictures of the poverty-stricken. The poor have their pride and feelings as we all have. In one instance, when a Head Start college student arrived in the community of Bridgewater to work on a project assignment, he promptly took a picture of a front yard of one of the low-income families; a home I had been visiting and where I established a rapport with the children and parents. The picture found its way into a Boston newspaper, much to the chagrin of the family at whose home the picture was taken. I soon was getting repercussions from the lady of the house, "how dare these people are allowed to come in here and start taking pictures without us knowing it!" I had to agree with her and reassured her that nothing of the sort will ever happen while I am in their midst.

While volunteers were attempting to perform community development-type tasks, their assignments often did not connect together for well-planned results. True, what volunteers accomplished was good to some degree; it was often offset by unanticipated and weakened circumstances. Some volunteers may have been used for office work or teacher aides which should have been the position of paid employees. Some volunteers came into VISTA not knowing "what in the world I am going to do;" working at some menial task or project or staying at home knitting! To solve any problem, one must become aware of the knowledge a problem exists.

Many failed to realize low-income people have wants and desires the same as middle-class families. The needs stem not so much by what they lack, as from what their neighbors have. Poor people must be made to feel wanted and helped and encouraged to take part in community undertakings.

As with the first-ever 4-H club in Bridgewater, disadvantaged youngsters had little experience in making decisions such as selecting project work, planning and conducting meetings or being an officer of a group. The lack of resources to carry out project work was a major problem with many families, therefore, an undertaking requiring a minimum of resources has been designed and offered. Being simple enough, the youngsters could carry them to completion, developing self-confidence and new experiences. To overcome the problem of insufficient resources, private funds were used (individual donations and my own pocket donations) to furnish some of the materials such as new wood, paint, scissors, sewing and cooking equipment. With those items provided, no young person was left out because they didn't have the money to buy materials. Items were also solicited from lumber yards, craft supply stores, florists and various organizations, with help from the leaders themselves.

"Laws grind the poor and the rich men rule the law," Oliver Goldsmith complained in the eighteenth century. Many poor people agreed that things haven't changed much. From the large cities, the O.E.O.'s young attorneys were taking the fight against poverty off the streets and into the courtrooms, where the poor never had much voice. Through the O.E.O.'s Legal Aid services, attorneys were making such disturbing waves that a State Senator felt compelled to "calm the waters" with an amendment to weaken the impact of the Legal Aid services operations by giving State Governors veto power over any part of the O.E.O. program. The amendment died quietly in a Senate-House conference committee after passing in the Senate. So, the budding O.E.O. program had a chance in the Nation's courts.

In one large city, for example, the program found a friend in the Bar Association and among individual attorneys. Common to each of the cities and small villages where an O.E.O. office was operating was the clientele . . . they were all poor. An O.E.O. official in Washington said thousands of legally indigent persons were receiving top-grade legal advice, equalizing situations where before they used to be helpless. The poor in the past never got equal protection under the law; it was only a theory and in practice, the system never worked that way.

The O.E.O. attorneys were fighting to battle urban renewal but when you eliminate the housing of four thousand citizens, most of them old and all of them poor, there must be some other place for them to re-locate. One Legal Aid attorney was arguing, not against a one-thousand room luxury hotel and nine parking lots but against their construction at the cost of eliminating the homes of thousands with no replacement.

Typical of the outstanding results by the newly-formed O.E.O. Corps of Attorneys was a case of a thirty-five-year-old woman who found herself in a mental institution, the victim of red tape, indifference and criminal negligence. The Legal Aid attorneys discovered her missing and found where she was incarcerated, overturned several sections of the department who had her case and reinstated the woman, if not in her rightful place in society, at least in freedom. One of the things O.E.O. has done with its energetic lawyers and its indiscriminately enthusiastic VISTA Volunteers is putting people who were in sad neighborhoods into a more productive life.

As the VISTA years went by, VISTA Washington began to recruit low-income people from their own communities. In time, they had people who would be trained to help their neighbors bring the concept of community development closer together. It made them feel "we're in this together, let us help each other." Often, people can identify needs of the communities in which they live and can work together with providers on problematic solutions. Soon, the name was changed from VISTA to

Action . . . Communities in Action. Fewer eighteen and nineteen year-olds were being recruited. People with more powerful weapons were being recruited . . . mature volunteers with highly developed skills, more lawyers, city planners and engineers to help get self-help housing started; also more accountants, banking, finance and marketing specialists to help establish health centers and other medical facilities for the poor. O.E.O. also concentrated on recruiting more blacks who have grown up in the urban ghettos and rural hollows, who knew the frustrations, needs and capabilities of their people.

Volunteers from poor communities who had little education or professional experience were trained to provide unique and valuable services to their people and to themselves. The ultimate aim of the government's drive against poverty was once described in these words: to provide the young with the opportunity to learn, the able-bodied with the opportunity to work, the poor with the opportunity to live in decency and dignity. This program was much more than a beginning. Rather it was a commitment . . . a total commitment of determination and strength to undertake an attack on the problems of poverty.

During my first year as a VISTA Volunteer, a summary report was sent out to VISTAs in the field to get a more precise picture of how Volunteers perceived and evaluated experiences and to identify possible changes that should be made to make VISTA a more meaningful, responsible and productive program. There were many critical responses against the program especially from the younger VISTAs. Many did not realize, even after training, VISTAs needed to find their own projects; they complained of not enough support from VISTA sponsors and doubted about the value of the VISTA program to the people it was intended to serve. Many Volunteers believed our Nation had the capability of ending all its hunger problems in a year's time. I had to disagree with many of the complaints and reactions. The summary stated it would be tragic if VISTA were to allow itself to become a pacification agency to the young volunteers (and it could have).

In my assignment to Windsor County as a VISTA, I had one hundred percent support from my sponsors: University of Vermont Extension Service in Burlington and Windsor County Co-operative Extension Service in Woodstock, respectively. I was expected to give a report on my activities weekly to my immediate supervisor, Edward Goodhouse and provide a plan for possible future projects. I was in my mid-forties when I decided to apply to VISTA. I felt it was a satisfactory decision in my direction as I had work experience and general experience in home management, child care, nursing and the knowledge of the problems of the disadvantaged. After all, youth has its advantages . . . but experience definitely has its rewards.

As I think of that high mountain country, I begin to feel a tranquility of being in such a place . . . a place where masses of red trillium bloomed in the woods in the Springtime and many varieties of wild flowers and plants. Wildlife abounded in the forest: raccoon, squirrel, porcupine, chipmunk, darting into roadsides of New

England asters. A mother raccoon could be seen with her six young --- cute as buttons --- trailing behind, scooting out of the way along the mountain roads after dark. In the mountains in July, the days never seemed hot and nights were always cool. How good it was to breathe the bracing air, smell the evergreens, sit beside a cool, hillside stream or picnic on a wild-flowered meadow, with a panoramic view of valleys and green mountains.

My choice for one of the most exquisite pleasures was to wait for the first light of daybreak or moon-rise on the mountain top. No matter where the mountain range, I found my niche there. I love the hazy peaks and distant valleys and a drive along a back road with a boulder-studded, fast-flowing brook alongside is an unforgettable experience. Every turn provides a view to delight the eye; mountain tops wrapped in mist, deep valleys criss-crossed by glinting streams and country roads. I walked through the forests frequently, my salvation for gathering my thoughts and saving my sanity after a day's labors filled with emotion in my attempts to bring together my plans for another project making a supreme effort to accomplish what it was I planned.

In the woods, amongst cedars and deciduous trees and animal tracks, I listened to the "sounds of silence!" A voice within me stirred, coming to arouse my thoughts in this beautiful place. I came upon a dead, hollow log that once may have been the home of baby rabbits. I rested there a moment. In the silence, I had a feeling of being watched, goose bumps rose on my neck. A rabbit, dashing past as if shot from a gun. I held my breath, hoping to prolong the moment. For me, the sighting was pure pleasure but the rabbit got no such enjoyment from this encounter as he scurried out of sight. I walked on. Another vibration-like in the leaves and brush. It was nearing dusk and I still had several places to explore before reaching the road that would take me home. The sounds continued, this time louder and nearer in the brush. I see it! A white-tailed deer dashing out in front of me through the thicket; making its way across the road into the field of red clover. It was darker now and strange noises were still heard in this forest standing next to the roadway. I thought about what my friend Julia told me: she heard "bear moanings" during the night in the woods behind her home; the very woods holding me enchanted at that moment. As she explained it, "As the bear walk, they moan with every step." My steps quickened as thoughts of the bear stayed with me. It was still a half-mile walk before I would reach my home by way of the iron bridge crossing the Ottauquechee River across from my trailer home. Bear tracks were evident in this part of the state and I had no desire to encounter the 'track-owner' after dark! . . . or anytime. The full moon was about to make its appearance over the mountain top; a memorable sight as I hurried home. My key unlocked the door, a warm thought came over me as I made my way inside. Now, I must plan for tomorrow, a day that will inevitably bring many more interesting situations once again in my service as a VISTA.

CHAPTER VIII

A STRANGER'S EYES SEE THE CLEAREST

"Though we travel the world over to find the beautiful, we must carry it with us or we find it not."
                    Author unknown

Even though I was assigned with the Extension Service in an area surrounding Bridgewater, I found myself stepping over into another community of the county to help people in need. The families I would be visiting knew little about me. They knew someone from the government was amongst them but "they never did trust the Government." I was an outsider and they were suspicious of me. I heard murmurings: "Who are we to let a stranger run our lives." I knew little about them also except that they were poor. I had only a vague idea what I would be doing in that strange community; only knew what I wanted to do; help these people help themselves escape from poverty and home visiting had to be the way to begin.

Most homes in that community had running water but no central heating. Some had indoor sanitary facilities and threadbare clothing; all received surplus food. One home raised goats and as goats can become pets very easily, they allowed one to walk on the kitchen table picking up leftover scraps.

In my attempts to locate families, I found, on an isolated dirt road in the mountain, living in a school bus-trailer combination, a father, mother and four grade school children. From the beginning, the mother was reluctant to invite me into their home, so we visited on their doorstep; the children performing small antics in their child-like ways to draw my attention. Donated clothing filled the bus section of the home almost to the ceiling while the trailer was their living room and bedrooms.

I decided to make frequent visits to establish a rapport with the mother; possibly through the children. The narrow dirt driveway had a rather steep grade from the main gravel road; as a result it was almost impossible to make the grade with my car during Mud Season in the Spring. As a result, I parked near the main road and walked up the hill to the house. After the first few visits, the children became accustomed to see me coming up the hill and raced down with their well-worn red wagon bouncing over the rocks and ruts in the road. One day one of the children asked me, "Rose, would you like a ride in the wagon with us?" I answered, "I would like that, will you come too?" The older child responded, "Sit here in the middle and one of us will drive and Mike will sit in back to protect you." We piled into the wagon in the positions we were told and rode full speed down the wet, dirt driveway over the boulders and exposed roots until . . . the wagon began tilting with the full load and over we came, depositing everyone onto the muddy, rain-soaked ground, while their mother watched from her doorstep.

We sat there on the cold, wet ground for a long moment, laughing at our mishap, the children asking me over and over, "Rose, are you alright, are you alright?" We enjoyed many rides since that first time; the children always ready to give me a ride in their little red wagon.

Before long, the mother realized I was a friend and not someone trying to change their lives. She began inviting me into the house for a cup of tea and a cookie as she and her children and I sat around the old round oak table in friendly conversation. Times such as those made me very happy to know and realize I have succeeded in making a friend. She got up the courage one day to ask if I would drive her to the rummage sale in the village. As we rode along, with the children in the back seat, sitting very quietly and mannerly, we talked about school problems and the difficulty they have in getting around without a car for transportation. It was then I asked if she would be interested in applying for a Home Nursing course I was planning. She accepted most graciously, coming through the class with flying colors, accepting a job as a nurse aide in a local nursing home besides doing private duty as a caregiver for a gentleman with a terminal illness; at the same time wanting to work more steadily in the nursing field.

I knew for some time there was something she wanted to say to me but I continued to be a friend and didn't push her. Then one day, as I sat with her and her children around the old oak table, she said, "Rose, I have something to tell you. Now that I know you better I can say it." She continued, "From the beginning, I didn't know if I could trust you because I thought you were in our community to take our children away." What a shocking thought! I hugged her and assured her it was not one of my duties and I had no reason to do anything of the kind. I felt great sorrow for this lady; in all these weeks I have been visiting the family, she must have had some emotional moments while the children and I were becoming buddies.

As I stated previously, we needed to establish a rapport with the families before we could even expect them to trust us and this incident was an excellent example. Her husband was a handyman by trade, a loner and a dump-picker by a persistent calling. He scoured the town dump every evening, rescuing treasures others needlessly threw away. He was always soft spoken, gentle and courteous. People said he was 'simple' but I doubt they ever got close enough to know. He may have considered *us* the simple ones . . . throwing things away that still had life left in them. He sought out and found the good we could not; in things and in people.

Their children were fun-loving and happy. The mother was solemn-faced but quick to smile; a neatly dressed lady who held a tight rein on running a household and proud of their home. Her husband enjoyed showing off his black stallion that he prized above all else. I saw him once, astride that giant, satiny horse . . . hatless, straight-backed, his hair smoothed down, his black riding boots up to his knees; so different he looked. He lifted his face into the wind, snapped the reins and rode off.

Passersby viewed their home as the dilapidated house but behind the dilapidated houses with their lilac bushes abloom and a rusted piece of machinery in the yard . . . there is a story; beautiful stories of families that called it home. A part of history, a part of life.

There was an obvious feeling of insecurity among the young people who had trouble developing self-confidence and appreciation for others. It was important, then, to recognize that certain projects were too highly structured for them. Still, the need was there for new experiences, recognition and response from others. I have discovered, the more frequently they interacted with one another, the stronger their friendship with others was likely to be. Making the initial contact with the low-income families was a major concern for me. My supervisor, Ed, was most helpful in presenting information on ways of 'opening the door' to these people. My knowledge of the home environment was the most important way to begin.

As one viewed an area, considered poverty-stricken, several environmental characteristics were readily seen. Buildings and homes were in a state of dilapidation, evidence of improvements or repairs were almost non-existent. This was especially true in the lower segment of low-income. There were poorly-kept yards, rotted or rotting porch floors and steps (sometimes lack of steps), broken window panes, deteriorated roofs. Most homes were usually small for the size of the family, some lacked furniture and what they did have was often in a poor state of repair. Many individuals held the belief that the low income were making all the progress of which they were capable and nothing could be done to help them help themselves. Should this have been true, we could have looked forward to the problem increasing rather than decreasing. However, considerable evidence showed this was not generally true; that a small percentage of those affected were victims of their heritage. It was true, in some cases, due to unbalanced diets and unsanitary conditions, the people seemed to have less energy and willingness to work.

Money was always a big problem. There was never enough of it. As one mother stated, "There's not much use in putting money aside when you just have to go right ahead and spend it." One exception was of a couple who shared the marketing as she explained it, "Me and him always do this together. I like to ask his opinion of what I get because when I go myself sometimes I spend too much. I carry a pencil and paper with me and add up the things as we go along. Then he tells when I have gotten to the amount he thinks I can spend."

It was November and hunting season was in progress. There were many red-coated, gun-toting hunters in the fields and woods, searching the countryside for the elusive white-tailed deer.

Driving along a blacktopped country road one frosty morning, I noticed a deer running across a field directly toward me; possibly frightened by gunshot. I was forced to stop in the center of the road to avoid hitting the big buck. There was light snow on the ground and the blacktop was icy. When he reached the road, he began slipping and sliding, falling to his knees, unable to get his bearings. I sat very still so as not to frighten him and to see how and if he could continue his journey; all the while hopeful another hunter would not be in sight of my remarkable observation. Soon another deer came dashing toward the highway in the path of the first one, slipping and falling as he reached the road. Following many antics, they finally got their bearings and dashed off into the foothills.

Deer are extremely vulnerable when hunting season arrives. Salt blocks are sometimes placed in strategic areas by hunters to entice the animals, as are tons of carrots, sugar beets and apples, where the deer then gather in herds to feed on some of their favorite foods, allowing the hunters to take a shot at them without having to move into the woodlands to locate one. Most states do not have a law against the practice, even though lawmakers and hunters have spoken out against the lack of sportsmanship exhibited when they attempt to lure an animal to a feeding station.

Christmas can be a sad season for homes with children. "Last year Santa promised me a talking doll, but when I awoke on Christmas morning there were no presents under the tree." A little girl had her hopes up and put faith in the red-coated joker, then found Santa Claus got into an accident or his reindeer got sick. Annie, age five, had every reason to believe in Santa Claus; she's seen him in stores and on television. Said one father, "We parents have to satisfy our childrens' minds in some way at some time. We know how kids feel when they don't get anything nice for Christmas . . . that's a hurtin' thing."

The feeling is typical of most families living in poverty. In a neighborhood where incomes are not always adequate to cover food and rent, parents who must deprive their children of new clothes and toys throughout the year, believe Christmas is a time when all children should be happy. There are many civic organizations, church groups and individuals who plan special Christmas projects to help families reach their goal of providing gifts for the children. "Sometimes the poor are suspicious when one gives them something," a social worker once said to me. "There are people out there having a deep, great pride. They don't want anybody to help them." Neighborhood residents were increasingly involved in distributing gifts, most saying they find the owners of grocery stores they patronize all year usually willing to make a contribution.

Annie's parents had a tree the following year and this time there was a talking doll under it. "It makes you short on something else and it hurts to look into my pocketbook sometime," the mother said, "but the children have to have it." To Annie's father, the year will probably bring another three hundred sixty-four days of poverty, including the obligation to complete payments on his childrens' toys. After Christmas . . . that can be a hurtin' thing.

Bridgewater natives sadly reminisced about the flood of nineteen hundred twenty-seven. In the middle of Winter that year, an electricity-charged rainstorm pounced upon the community bringing with it a deluge of rain. In Bridgewater Center, the Chatteauguay River flowed with all its physical power under an iron bridge between the dirt road and a one-room schoolhouse, where twenty children were taught their readin', 'ritin' and 'rithmetic in grades kindergarten through eighth.

The intense rainstorm continued for several days, causing the river to overflow its banks and with it the collapse of the bridge, trapping the teacher and children without an exit. Besides the rain, there was run-off from the mountains nearby. For three weeks, parents and neighbors came on foot, delivering food, medicine and clothing, braving the overflowing waters; until finally subsiding, releasing the teacher and children.

Imagine, if you can, the heroism and courage of the teacher; feeding, teaching and caring for the youngsters. The anxiety of the parents and the trust they were forced to place upon the teacher, who had no place to retreat for some rest and relaxation.

World Day of Prayer is held every March first throughout the world in every country, here and abroad. It is a call to worship, adoration, thanksgiving and peace in the world. Its theme in nineteen sixty-eight was "Bear one another's burden" (Galatians 6:2). As a VISTA Volunteer, I was asked to present the meditation, using the theme as my subject. A grateful audience attended my presentation, graciously accepting and recognizing my purpose in the community of Windsor County in Vermont.

CHAPTER IX

GROW WHERE YOU ARE PLANTED

"Ask not what your Country can do for you . . . but what you can do for your Country."

> President John Fitzgerald Kennedy
> in his inaugural address.

As I remember it, the day the money stopped was a dim vista for VISTA and this VISTA was no exception . . . the Day the headlines blared: AND NOW A WORD FROM YOUR SPONSORS, VISTA WASHINGTON: POVERTY PROGRAM GOING BROKE! POVERTY BILL FACES TOUGH BATTLE IN HOUSE! DIM VISTA FOR VISTAs! VISTA WORKERS VOW TO STAY ON DESPITE NO PAY!

The letters were coming to VISTA Washington; telegrams speeding back and forth: "As long as we can manage, we're going to stay because the poor must stay." "We're going to stick to our jobs." And to VISTA staff: "*We'll* stick it out, as long as *you* can."

Then a letter from VISTA Washington Director: *VISTA has another difficult task to ask of you . . .* began the letter; sent out to more than four thousand Volunteers in the field that November, nineteen hundred sixty-seven.

When the news broke, I've already had invitations for meals and food was brought to my door. Not all volunteers were quick to see a silver lining in the warning that Congress might not pass the O.E.O. continuing resolution in time for them to receiving their November fourteenth living allowance, but they saw it as a challenge to continue working amongst the poor.

I wasn't exactly sure *how* I'd stay "but stay I will!" The uncertain days that followed the announcement showed that the crisis might have been a good thing after all. I could often see positive results of the work that had been done; what I did not realize was how much my work had been noticed and how eager people were to repay a small measure of that help. Said one mother on welfare, "We ain't got much, but what we do have we'll share." Families across America did likewise; squeezing a little more to make an extra place at the table. In a Massachusetts community, an enraged group held a meeting to keep VISTAs in their midst. Thousands of New York residents planned demonstrations at the Statute of Liberty and on Wall Street. It was not just the poor that were concerned; however, phone companies offered to postpone billing of the VISTAs and an electric company offered free electricity. Landlords promised not to evict VISTAs who could not pay their rent.

With the specter of a payless November fourteenth looming, VISTAs began making emergency plans . . . families offered me a room in their home, "in case you need it." In one State, the Warden readied the City jail with an "open door policy" for needy VISTAs and promised to provide food and clothing.

Before my VISTA service, I worked as a Red Cross Gray Lady in various activities at the Traverse City State Hospital. Soon, I received a substantial check in the mail from my volunteer buddies. Rev. Ohmer Curtiss, Director of Volunteer Services at the hospital, offered financial help. My own mother from Michigan sent a check, "because you might need it." Business places, organizations, attorneys, local citizens, civic groups and colleges offered assistance to VISTAs across America. A Chicago newspaper led one story with, "it seems everyone loves VISTA Volunteers except their Government!" Despite the problems, VISTAs across the country were determined to stay on their jobs no matter what the 'cost' . . . to continue to work until all sources of revenues were exhausted and then some.

It was my deep desire to serve the poor and nothing was going to stop me now, "because I cared." I AM A VISTA VOLUNTEER, I WILL REMAIN A VISTA VOLUNTEER AND WILL DWELL WITH MY FRIENDS AT BRIDGEWATER CORNERS, VERMONT!

The check finally arrived in early December with an expression of gratitude from VISTA Washington!

My VISTA work continued to be a challenge but I found happiness in everything I did with and for my people. As I was in my late-forties when I decided on becoming a VISTA, to pay a significant role in the War On Poverty, it has given me a wonderful opportunity to 'do something with my life' . . . an ambition to get out there and be a part of this great Nation . . . to use my talents, my time and my treasures; with experience enabling me to perform a variety of services for poor people of all ages.

Thanksgiving Day arrived, my first in Vermont as a VISTA. I was invited to my supervisor Ed's house for dinner with his wife, Gene, and their two children. At the last minute, I had to cancel the dinner invitation due to heavy rain which found its way through the ceiling of my trailer home and onto the living room floor. Emptying buckets in quick succession was the order of the day; as many as I could find amongst my meager cache of utensils to catch the 'water falls' as they came down walls and ceilings. The rain continued most of the day and night that Thanksgiving Day and it was becoming evident that I would need to find another place to live soon. To top it off, I was notified my rent was being raised double. As the roof needed replacing and frequent Fall rains were causing a deluge of water inside, I could not spend time at home emptying buckets whenever it rained; I had to be about my VISTA ministrations! If I wanted to break even in my living expenses, I would need to look for another place.

An informant of the community told me of a small house available for rent in Bridgewater Center, two miles into the mountains . . . tucked away from the busy highway, in a beautiful valley beside a fast-flowing stream. The landlord owned Hubbard's Grocery next door and was happy that someone would finally be living there. It was a dream-come-true for me! I would be living nearer to 'my people' for whom I was there to serve.

It was December, my son, Tom, was visiting me from Michigan. What a coincidence and a convenience now that he was here to help me move into the humble little house in the valley.

My new home had a twenty-by-twenty-foot living room; a corner of which I could use for my office, a small bedroom, tiny kitchen with a combination wood and gas range for cooking, sink, table and two chairs. A one-piece bathroom stood in one corner of the house. There was no hot water nor lavatory. The house was heated with a bottled-gas radiant heater in the living room and a small wall gas heater in the kitchen. The living room walls were of brown plywood; that didn't help to make the interior any lighter but I didn't mind; I loved the tiny house situated next to the beautiful stream just outside my back door, with mountains looming on either side. An old round oak table stood in the living room making a very large desk on which to work. The front steps to the house were of Vermont marble; usual for many homes in the East in place of concrete or brick. A marble quarry is located some forty miles West.

Many families have mountain spring water piped into their homes and as the natives said, "Spring water requires no water softeners. By the time it travels over the many rocks found in the mountains, there is no hardness left." The water is piped directly from the mountain spring and must be keep running from the faucet during the cold Winter months to keep it from freezing. No one seems to mind leaving the faucet running; it uses no electricity.

New England Winters become very cold, as I have accidentally discovered shortly after moving into my new home in the Center. A newly-found friend gave me a cutting from one of her house plants, kept in a small glass of water to hasten rooting. One morning I awoke and shivered, saying to myself, "Why does it feel so cold this morning? Must have been a cold night." I jumped out of bed and walked into the living room. BRRR! The gas heater was cold, the water holding my plant was frozen solid, the thermometer in the room read thirty degrees! "What's going on?" The gas tanks went dry! The gas delivery truck, expected the previous day, became so busy filling other's tanks, he didn't have time for more deliveries. I soon discovered the gas was not only out in the living room heater but the tank serving the kitchen was so nearly empty, it was barely burning. I dressed quickly, putting on long johns, heavy socks, two sweaters, wool jacket, snow pants and boots. At the same time, thinking 'I can always go out to the car to keep warm before the gas man comes.' Lo and behold! the car wouldn't start. I had no wood on hand to use in the kitchen stove. WHAT TO DO??? The delivery truck would not arrive until late afternoon. The service station was so flooded with calls due to the minus-forty degrees and wouldn't get to start my car until evening. I spent part of the morning with my landlady next door then walked a half-mile down the road to a friend's house. The warmth of her home was comforting to me but I couldn't stay long, just in case someone would come to start my car. I had no electric heater and longed for an electric blanket. The gas delivery was made at three o'clock and soon after I got my car started.

Next day a parcel arrived for me at the Post Office. Surprise of surprises! An electric blanket from Mom. Believe me, I would have crawled under it for the remainder of the day and night, had it arrived the day of the freeze. Nevertheless, it was much appreciated for the rest of the long, cold Winter.

Now that I was cozily situated in my comfortable little home, I awakened the first few nights, thinking: how unusual for it to be raining every night, only to discover it was the beautiful, lazy little stream whispering to me just beyond my back door. It was a God-send for me to stroll along the edge of the water when Spring arrived; if only to ease my homesickness I was feeling after my son left for his home in Michigan. As I maneuvered my car one late afternoon along the icy road leading home, I couldn't help thinking that my first Christmas in Vermont . . . without tree or decorations . . . was going to be the loneliest of my life. Away from family and Mom, I did what some people do when they're lonely . . . I had a good cry!

As I sat alone on the edge of my bed, I heard footsteps coming up my front steps. Trying to compose myself, I rose and walked to the door. Before the visitor had a chance to knock, I had the door opened. What a pleasant surprise . . . a Christmas tree! As the cabin had an empty flower pot sitting next to the old sewing machine, the tree was neatly placed into it surrounded by moss and rocks to hold it upright. What are we going to use for decorations? No problem! As we gathered as many cooking utensils, forks, knives and spoons as we could find in the meager cache of supplies, the tree was soon beginning to look alive and ready for the day of Christ's birth. I then found several bracelets, pins and necklaces to give it just a touch of sparkle; all being attached with dental floss. At the top we placed an eggbeater disguised as an angel with an aluminum-foil skirt, wings and halo. I spun around to hug this dear friend who came as an 'angel of mercy.' "You've just taught me a thing or two about the spirit of Christmas. Thanks to you, this will be the best ever." In another couple of days, a neighbor stopped in to invite me to their home for Christmas dinner; a family with five children who wanted to share with this stranger a part of their lives; this Christmas, what turned out to be *one* of my happiest in this beautiful area of Bridgewater.

A river bank was an exciting source of play for Steve, an active six-year-old who loved doing 'conservation work' in the fast-flowing, partially ice-covered stream across the snow-covered dirt road from his home. On a cold, February afternoon with a brisk, North wind and snowflakes in the air, the river ran deep, almost overflowing in places from the melting snow of a week ago and run-off from the mountains nearby.

On this particular day, hatless, he wore a light tee shirt and pants with his knees sticking out, a shabby coat minus buttons and on his feet were unlaced shoes minus stockings. The temperature was ten degrees above zero in mid-afternoon. He liked watching the water under the ice, flowing steadily, poking it rhythmically with his newly-found stick. What fun it was . . . checking out different areas of the icy river, breaking up the ice as he went along.

He played alone and enjoyed wandering off by himself along the river bank. His mother caught a glimpse of him occasionally from the kitchen window. When she could see him no longer behind the bushes, growing along the river and dusk was settling in, she walked out onto the porch and called to Steve to come home. "Stevie, come home. It's getting dark." "He must have gone father down the river to play," she thought to herself. She waited for the sound of his footsteps on the porch. Coatless, she walked to the road, calling, "Steve, Steve, come home." Still, no answer from the little boy at the river. "Where is he, I ain't see him for some time," she said to herself. A neighbor was notified. Word spread quickly. "Steve is missing. Has anyone seen him?" "Yes, someone saw him about an hour ago playing on the river bank with a stick."

Whole families were outdoors in the cold, clear dusk of the evening, searching in the close-knit neighborhood. No one could locate the little boy. Grandmas and

Grandpas were concerned, as they searched, "Where could that little child have gone off to on this extremely cold night, we must find him. Could he have wandered too far and lost his way home?" His home was located in a small settlement of homes of the elderly and young families. It is where I also lived in my small cabin, one mile down the road, near an extension of that same river.

As I was preparing a 4-H project in my home, I was unaware of the excitement taking place just down the road from me. Suddenly, I heard a frantic knock at my door. I ran to answer it. "Rose, can you come quick? Stevie was found floating with the swift current face down under the ice. He is just now being taken home and they need you." I grabbed a couple blankets and my hot water bottle, jumped into my car and raced down the snow-covered dirt road to Steve's house. I found him lying on the couch in the living room in a semi-comatose condition, an old coat wrapped around him, his face ashen and his skin blue, with shallow and labored breathing. I instructed his mother to heat some water quickly in her castiron kettle and heat some rocks from the shed on her wood-burning kitchen stove and put several towels and blankets in the oven 'but watch them carefully so they don't catch on fire.' We had no access to a heating pad but were able to improvise with what we had at hand, along with my hot water bottle and blankets. After drying him off, we wrapped him in warm blankets and tucked the warmed rocks in the towels around his body to keep him continuously warm. Talking to him constantly, I didn't leave his bedside.

Many of the homes in the neighborhood had no phone making it impossible to get in touch with a doctor. When he opened his eyes and began to respond to verbal communication, warm drinks were offered to him. And when he was becoming more alert and I thought it safe to leave him in the care of his mother. I returned to my home to phone the doctor for instructions. Steve was going to be fine. Again , I returned to his home and found him still lying on the couch, smiling at me when I walked in (I whispered a prayer of thanksgiving). I gave his mother further instructions from the doctor: warm liquids to drink when awake, keep him warm and make sure the house is kept warm.

Steve was found under the ice approximately a half-mile from his home when a searching neighbor saw a dark shadow under the ice and plucked him out; having difficulty reaching him due to the swift current and large boulders where his jacket caught, preventing him from floating farther down the river. A miracle! I remained at his home for several hours while he slept. When he awoke, he said to me, "I stepped on the ice because my stick fell in and I had to get it back." Next morning, I returned to check on him and his family. Stevie excitedly ran to greet me, jumping into my arms, telling me how he fell into the water and couldn't find his way out from under the ice. In the same breath he informed me, "I'm going back there again today when I find a new stick." I didn't doubt him!

CHAPTER X

THE GRAND OL' PATRIARCH

"It is not I who speaks, but life within me who has much to say."
　　　　　　　　Unknown

A Credit Union National Association (C.U.N.A.) representative contacted me regarding the possibility of forming a credit union at the Bridgewater Woolen Mill.

In present-day America, a credit union can be as important as a birth certificate. It is the key that opens the door to low-interest loans, a mortgage on a home, the purchase of a car. And it is as unavailable to the poor as are many other things middle-class America takes for granted. I first learned credit unions can be set up in low-income communities, while in VISTA training.

I recruited families, business people and other interested villagers who might be receptive to the idea.

A get-together was arranged at the Bridgewater Elementary School for a C.U.N.A. representative to explain the concept to woolen mill workers and those who have taken an interest in the possibility of forming a credit union; e.g., local residents, business owners, low-income people and the Vermont Credit Union Director, who explained that the money they put in would be like personal savings, collecting dividends from interest paid on loans. I emphasized to them this would be a project they would eventually run themselves and I would only act as advisor, until another is found.

Many questions were presented but the people were saying, "How can we save and have money to put in when we already know where the money must go before we even earn it? There is food to buy, the car needs fuel and nothing else left to do anything with." The concerns of the folk wasn't exactly the makings of a solution toward establishing a credit union.

Many more meetings were held at which there were only a handful of interested residents. Progress was held up due to lack of interest and it was decided that plans be tabled until such a time we can bring it up again. Time passed and rumors flew that Bridgewater Woolen Mill was going to close. Employees were going to find jobs in Ludlow, twelve miles south, or Rutland, twenty miles west. We heard repercussions, "I'll have to go on welfare. What kind of jobs are available for us to do? We have no formal training in any other jobs. Who will want us? When we move to another town and another job, then we may have a credit union there."

The idea of Credit Unions is actually very old. All one need do is to convince those who can best profit by it, to get together and start but they should not get the impression that a lot of money will be available in a short period of time. With proper interest, credit unions can build up the strength of the poor.

In talking with several women in regard to projects, many expressed a wish to learn all about Home Nursing. I began recruiting women (and men, if interested). I found women willing to volunteer their time and services to assist in the class, presenting their expertise in various aspects of teaching. Six women applied for the free six-week course, held in the Bridgewater Elementary School one evening weekly. A mannequin was needed on which the students were required to practice their clinical experience. Where to find one? Can you guess who was chosen? . . . much to the enjoyment of the class members.

The sessions included demonstrations of folding paper bags for refuse, hand-washing before beginning their work with the patient, wrist testing of liquids, feeding the helpless patient, vital signs (temperature, pulse, respirations), making a back-rest with a chair, body mechanics, oral care, how's and why's of a bath (and actually bathing their mannequin!), transferring, turning a patient, bed making, cold compresses, improvising and bandaging were some of the aspects of teaching. A talk was presented on well-balanced diets by a Nutritionist from the University of Vermont. Presentations were given by nurses, Mrs. Camp and Mrs. Doten, both of Woodstock. A doctor visited with information on child-care and when to call the doctor. A text book was provided by the UVM Extension Service for each student, free to charge. At the close of the course, certificates were handed out to each student supplied by Elm Tree Press without cost.

As a result of the knowledge gleaned from the Home Nursing class, a student applied for a class in Practical Nursing for the following term at a regional hospital and was accepted. Another student received a job as a Nurse Aide at a local nursing facility. Others prepared to use their knowledge in home situations until suitable jobs could be found. A note of interest: the low-income woman mentioned in a previous chapter who began caring for a gentleman with a terminal illness continued to work as a Nurse Aide in a foster home setting.

My VISTA days march on and I am involved in many projects, making new friends, meeting more people; having a wonderful rapport with so many who were once strangers. I soon had to decide whether I would re-enroll for another year of service with VISTA. Thoughts of home and children were tugging at me. Mother was getting up in years and alone at home except for my children and her friends and neighbors who were good to her. How can I leave my friends here?

I continued to be an intermediary between the helping services and the poor. Transportation continued to be an everlasting problem. There were times I wasn't sure of my position; so many people requested transportation and at a time when I needed to get to another appointment, meetings to be held, helping services contacted. How can I spread myself so thin? . . . decisions to be made, problems to attempt to solve, spouses having marital problems, medical emergencies occurring among families.

As an example of how my VISTA work was becoming wide-spread: I had a phone interview with VISTA Washington for the *American Journal of Nursing* on "Volunteering: How it Affects the Nursing Profession." It was to be published in a future issue of the periodical.

Regardless of the physical strength required of a VISTA, I have had to spend time in bed occasionally due to ills. Whenever that inconvenience occurred, there was always someone at my door bringing me food or just stopping by to check on me. I think Someone demanded of me to take time off for some rest and relaxation every so often to renew my energy to 'fly again' in my ministrations to others.

Webster's dictionary defines a mine as a large excavation made in the earth from which to extract metallic ores as coal, gold and others. Gold is defined as a precious metal used in coins and jewelry, among other alloys; a heavy, yellow, metallic chemical element; bringing me to a gold mine.

Centuries ago have seen a definite scramble to see who would be first to stake a claim to a certain piece of land that was found to have a guarantee of finding that golden vein for which men fought. On a hike into the mountains, it was not difficult to locate the exact spot where a mine had been dug due to the huge pile of tailings, left behind when digging was accomplished.

In my travels, I had an opportunity to meet a grand ol' patriarch of ninety years young: Harold Perkins, who knew every tree in those beautiful Green Mountains surrounding Bridgewater, in the center of which he made his home and who farmed the land before Nature took over, returning it to the forest.

He asked me one morning in May, "Rose, how would you like to visit an old abandoned gold mine?" I definitely could not pass up an opportunity of a lifetime! On our trek up the mountain-side, he showed me old cellar holes surrounded by stone fences so expertly laid without mortar or any other sort of material to hold the rocks together, but now, centuries later, falling to ruin. They are truly a living legend to the hard work the families placed there to gather the rocks from the cleared fields in preparation for tilling, to provide a living. Frequently, one can find a grave site by the many stones placed in small, neat piles or laid to separate a garden spot from the door-yard or to line a cellar hole after it had been dug.

After what seemed like a mile walk from our car, parked along the roadside, a large pile of tailings came into view and we knew, somewhere nearby, was the old abandoned mine. We saw what appeared to be a large opening into the earth surrounded by pine logs laid one on top of the other, to resemble a shack at first but ended there to become a tunnel. Pine and deciduous tree seedlings were growing atop the tunnel now; a rotting, squeaky wooden door was swinging in the wind by one deerskin hinge. We approached the mine cautiously; a tunnel approximately six feet high by eight feet wide greeted us as we entered a space of complete darkness.

A flashlight we brought along became a real necessity now, because as Harold announced, "A bear may have used this space for his Winter's den and may not be finished with his nap!" Ever so slowly, we made our way into the darkness of the tunnel, stumbling over rocks laying at our feet, water dripping from the sod roof onto our heads produced by the mountain springs, underfoot became a mudpath. The veins of gold removed, though some still evident, Harold, pointing to other veins, remarked there were still traces of the precious ore but not worth the effort for mining. Slowly making our way into the mine, we stopped frequently to listen for sounds from within. We stopped suddenly to stare at the ground . . . BEAR TRACKS! "Which direction are they heading?" Luckily, toward the outdoors.

By now, having traveled approximately a hundred feet, we continue on our way. I am told fascinating stories of affluent mining towns during the gold rush where men 'fought for their rights.' Towns of five hundred population or less suddenly increased to thirty thousand. Railroads were built to serve the mining camps, hotels constructed to house the miners. One particular town boasted of sixty saloons during the gold rush. Some mining areas in the East were constructed with superior skills; huge buildings surrounding the mining entries while others were a hole in the ground.

On another walk into the mountain during the Winter, while stopping to tie my boot, a small spot of water caught my eye. The water was surrounded by a huge snowdrift. Approaching it slowly and picking up a long twig, I poked it into the water. I dropped the twig. It disappeared suddenly, continuing to bubble for what seemed like a long minute. I knew then, I discovered an old mine consisting only of a hole in the ground. I did not linger!

The path underfoot was becoming muddier with every step, as we found our way over pebbles and larger boulders to prevent slipping into the mud holes. The golden veins continued to run along the rock walls and it shall never be known for what distance the tunnel would have taken us. To continue the trip would be inviting a possible confrontation with the bear who may be returning to finish his Winter's nap. We decided it wise to slowly make our way back to civilization.

To have known and listened to Harold's memorable experience of the past and his knowledge of the world around him was an experience I shall never forget. I have walked a path of history!

Harold then told me about a Vermonter who, in the late eighteen hundreds, rigged a camera to a microscope and started taking pictures of snowflakes on his farm. In nineteen thirty-one he published his book, *Snow Crystals*, with twenty-four hundred black and white photos. Naturally, no two were alike.

CHAPTER XI

SAND FLEAS AND WILD ANIMALS

"A part of wisdom is to know the value of now . . . before it is gone forever."

As people helping other people, VISTAs' main concern had to be with feelings and attitudes. In our VISTA training experiences, we discovered actions based solely on our *own* feelings or attitudes have generally produced damaging results.

In order to gain concern for the poor, we had to learn some things and make adjustments in our own way of living. This was easier for some of us than for others. In the process, we learned basic principles of the lives of the poor that we had to remember if we were to 'get our programs together.' In reality, we had to think for ourselves; to face problem situations for what they were. Sometimes we had help from our training supervisor, other times we had to struggle through it alone. As we fumbled our way through, we faced obstacles in the form of decisions, adjustments and even persons in our class that tended to make the going difficult. Unless our primary motive was to be of service and benefit to the people and community in which we served, we might as well have packed our bags and left.

The 4-H members and I had many positive and productive round-table discussions at my home concerning their projects. Once, in the midst of our hands-on activities in the craft project, the conversation led to camping and how they traveled with their parents to a certain spot in the mountains. Suddenly, one of the girls spoke, "Why can't *we* go sometime?" Another member responded,"And why *can't we*?" A spark kindled and soon we were planning a camping trip. Parental permissions granted, camping and food equipment borrowed, supplies purchased, our plans were finalized for a weekend trip to the top of a mountain.

Have you ever gone on a camping trip with five active thirteen-year old girls, where the only noises you hear are the girls and the animals?

We picked a spot on three-thousand-seven-hundred-twenty-foot Shrewsbury Mountain, between Plymouth and Rutland, seven miles from our homes; an isolated area that was almost too good to be true (we thought); away from the hustle and bustle of civilization.

It was to be a weekend campout, Friday through Sunday. My roommate, Dorothy, would drive us to the spot and return home to continue with her projects. Excitement was at its height as we arrived at our campsite. We began unloading our supplies, sleeping bags, ice chest, insect repellent, towels and soap, water jugs, a kerosene lantern and flashlight, Band-aids, beverages and food, while Dorothy left with the car.

This site on Shrewsbury Mountain was constructed sixty years ago by President Roosevelt's Civilian Conservation Corps, who built cabins, roads and bridges and cut ski trails throughout America for public use. This particular site consisted of hiking trails, children's playground, ball field, picnic spot and a beautiful, snug, stone and log five-room cabin with a fieldstone fireplace, partitioned rooms, covered patio attached to one side of the building, glassed and barred windows (though many were lacking glass then). Another patio was built outdoors with a three-foot high stone wall encircling a picnic table and grill ... all this located in the center of a green meadow covered with red clover and goldenrods. No water nor electricity was available.

We walked in to inspect the interior of the cabin and discovered it was also being used by the animals of the forest nearby. While I debated the unlikeliness of us sleeping inside the cabin, I decided to wait; to ponder that decision later with the girls. Inside the cabin were notes from other campers expressing their appreciation "for its use" and for "being the first one to use the new flue pipe on this old stove." There was even advice on how to start a fire, "keep the damper open all the way and crack the door about an inch." There were notes of reminiscence: "It's amazing that something 'this cool' could remain from year to year." "A calm night; no wind howling."

After inspecting every nook and cranny around the meadow and surrounding area, the girls decided they would like to take a dip in the reservoir. Dusk was setting in and there was two miles of forest to walk through to get to the swimming hole. We placed our heavy, cardboard supply box on the picnic table inside the cabin and more supplies on the table outdoors in another cardboard box. Then we were off . . . half running down the mountain road, singing and enjoying the great outdoors. What great swimming on this beautiful evening with the pondfrogs serenading us in their deepest sopranos. It is said, 'time goes fastest when you're having fun' and before we realized, darkness was upon us, and time to head back to camp. This time, we walked in total darkness with everyone telling their own versions of ghost stories.

We approached the campground with a feeling of abandonment. "LISTEN, DO YOU HEAR WHAT I HEAR?" I announced. "Noises in the cabin. Could an animal have sneaked in while we were away?" As it was already dark, we decided it wouldn't be wise to disturb whatever it was gnawing away at something, which, no doubt, was our cardboard box. As we sat around the campfire, eating sandwiches and watermelon by the light of the kerosene lantern; two girls were planning on sleeping inside the cabin anyway, "even if it isn't fit for humans." "But there was an animal in it and we didn't have the slightest idea what sort of animal and I wasn't about to find out at this point." We discussed it and said, "If it is a porcupine, they can become fierce if disturbed. They are gnawing animals, three feet long, having coarse hair mixed with long, stiff, sharp spines; not something I care to encounter in a small space. If it's a pohl cat (skunk), well, you know what he can do to us and our friends, our neighbors, our parents, our animals; they are not fussy when it comes to attacking. And if . . . a larger animal????" Well, we ran out of 'ifs' and finally discouraged anyone who had the slightest thought of entering the cabin. We would sleep in the open air tonight!

We agreed upon a grassy spot, near the outdoor patio; not fifty feet from the forest. Spreading our sleeping bags on the soft earth (?), we settled in for the night, as the gnawing continued inside the cabin. As we lay in perfect contentment and agreement that this was indeed a wonderful idea to camp here on this most beautiful mountain, no matter that an animal *was* near or even if we *were* prevented from entering the cabin . . . wasn't it nice to have the privilege to sleep under the stars (what stars?) with no one to disturb us. FAMOUS WORDS! UNTIL . . . as we lay in our sleeping bags the animals in the forest began calling with their mysterious sounds; the crunching of leaves beneath the footsteps of creatures on the forest floor and the fierce screeching of the raccoons from their hiding places sending shivers up our spines! The cloud-filled sky with resonating sounds of far-away thunder and the constant gnawing of the animal in the cabin made us all wish we had earplugs to turn it all off. But, wasn't it wonderful to be free? Out here with all the animals? I said to myself,

"Must be the beastly mosquitoes that are so bothersome. Maybe a storm is brewing." The girls' voices gradually subsided one by one until all were asleep, *except me*. WHAT IS THAT SOUND OF FOOTSTEPS I HEAR, THEY ARE TOO CLOSE FOR COMFORT!!!

On that pitch-black night, I tried to dismiss my frightful thought. The gnawing continued, the screeching of the coons grew louder, the crunching of the leaves more frequent, the thunder booms nearer. As I lay there on the warm grass that July, nineteen hundred sixty-seven; unable to sleep, imaginative thoughts were racing through my head: I knew porcupine can become fierce when disturbed, how will we get him to leave in the morning (that is, if we survive the night) and if indeed it *is* a porcupine chewing up our box. What other large animal could it be? My thoughts were of lightning bolts and rain pelting down on us, attacks by an unknown animal or the owner of those footsteps I keep hearing.

My watch read one o'clock A.M. I had not yet closed my eyes in sleep. I believe I heard every movement and sound in that mountain. Emotions got the best of me as I lay awake and after so many years, my thoughts still go back to Shrewsbury Peak; after which the Town of Shrewsbury, Vermont, is named, and our camping expedition.

Shrewsbury was a small village surrounded by farming country; as I remember it, midst a jumble of boulders, dwarf wildflowers scattered across the barren land as if fallen off a rainbow; with lichen embossed on rock outcroppings. I think of having driven a road through this countryside many times, on my travels to visit the underprivileged living there. As I drove on, I could hear the sound of a waterfall in the mountain and knew there was more than that which met my eye. I passed mountain streams flowing in all their glory . . . to get a sense of what my wooded valley in Vermont may have been like so many thousands of years before; after the glaciers left New England. Lupines, Mountain Laurel and Indian Paint Brush were growing and blooming on this mountain. The wind hummed a gentle melody as it stirred the leaves of the sugar maple; so numerous here along with beech, conifers and white birch leaning heavily; with its shallow root system hardly preventing it from falling. It is a place where I thrilled at the thought of stopping my car to absorb the beauty of the silhouettes of the distant mountains; Pico and Killington. It was also close to all this beauty of Shrewsbury that held smells and sounds for which I was not prepared, as I lay awake that dark night on top of that same mountain . . . a mountain where the United States Government built this cabin of stone and wood for us, the public, and which we were unable to use on our camping adventure due to the carelessness of other campers and vandals. How sad, there are people who thrill at the thought of spoiling a wild and beautiful spot.

It was three o'clock A.M. and the sky began to show signs of daybreak. In due time, the sounds of the night grew fainter, the thunder claps stopped gradually, footsteps became quieter . . . it was now time for the *animals* bedtime

. . . thank you! By daybreak everyone awakened at the same time. BUT . . . why is everyone scratching so much? OH NO, IT CAN'T BE TRUE, WE ARE BEING INVADED BY SAND FLEAS! I reached for the insect repellent and began spraying. They were in our hair, on our skin, in our clothing. One girl became hysterical from the itching which finally abated but not before all of us were extremely uncomfortable. After a good rub-down with towels and a change of clothing, we, at last, found relief. Breakfast was prepared from which we were able to find enjoyment in that sunlit meadow. Now for the big decision on who was going to remove the animal from the cabin. Everyone pitched in; the girls yelling and screaming, while running around the building striking the sides of the cabin, when suddenly Mr. Porky made his entrance in the doorway. Stopping for a long moment to carefully inspect his surroundings, he ambled out into the woods . . . no doubt whispering to himself, "Never again will I come near those noisy girls."

Despite a cloud-filled night with threat of a storm that moved elsewhere, the day dawned bright with sunrise greeting us through the forest across the meadow. Not only did the rain stay away, we were instrumental in freeing ourselves from the porcupine and sand fleas and keeping the creatures of the forest at a distance. We may never know how close we may have come to a larger animal on that pitch-black night. Porky chewed the corner of the heavy box completely out even though none of the material was found, proving he had himself a delicious midnight snack.

The girls admitted our campout was exciting and fun but they were sure they didn't want to spend another night. As Dorothy was to pick us up on Sunday afternoon, it was only Saturday morning, and she had no way of knowing we cancelled our plans for another night. As a result, following breakfast, we secured our supplies in another box and started off for a walk to one of the girl's parents' home, five miles away! There we met Dorothy, who drove us back to pick up the supplies. As we were returning to our homes one of the girls inquired, "Can we do this again sometime?" I wasn't sure everyone agreed but they all admitted it was a campout they will not soon forget.

As I re-told our experiences to several residents later, a gentleman remarked, "Do you really mean you camped outdoors up on Shrewsbury? Why, that is the place someone saw a mountain lion not long ago!!! I had to believe he was not kidding.

Incidentally, I hoped to visit 'our' cabin a year ago while visiting Vermont. Instead, I received the shocking news that it burned to the ground. Taking a drive up Shrewsbury to see for myself, I found, to my sadness and disappointment, the remnants of the outdoor stone patio and the tall fireplace chimney standing alone.

CHAPTER XII

A HAPPY VISTA

"Whatever hour you are blessed with, take it with grateful hands."

My 'year toward tomorrow' would soon be ending and I made my decision to re-enroll for another year. The VISTA program was set up for VISTA Volunteers to remain at a site for a year; more if they chose to re-enroll. That was my wish because there were many projects that needed to continue. I would be leaving my work site for a two-week leave before returning to continue the work for my people of Windsor County, Vermont.

Upon my return, I hoped to do more research in programs for the younger residents and work closely with the Extension Service in areas of health education for the low-income population. There were many loose ends to tie up before I could take my leave, along with getting new projects in the planning stages.

As time went on, people were still learning about my work. Through a radio interview at WNHV in New Hampshire, a gentleman heard my talk and became interested in joining VISTA. A lady who had a parent in the nursing home where the Geri-Teens worked, wanted to begin volunteering, too.

The Geri-Teens began making aprons, bib-style, to wear in their nursing home assignments, assisted by a 4-H clothing leader. Materials were being donated by various organizations. The craft project grew to two separate groups and soon another woodworking group was about to be formed.

On March twentieth, a year following my arrival, I boarded a plane at Burlington National Airport for a two-week vacation at my home in Michigan. Another 'Happy Birthday' to have the opportunity, once again, to see my family after more than a year's absence. How good to see Mom, my children, Judy, Tom and Nancy, my grandsons, Brian, age three and one-half and a new baby, Joel, age one year, all on hand to welcome me home. It was a beautiful two weeks being home again and catching up on news happenings, visiting friends and co-workers. Before long, I found myself on the jet plane winging my way back across the hills and valleys and plains bringing me back to my 'other families' in Vermont and to begin another 'year toward tomorrow.' My home visits resumed, projects continued and new areas of interest researched.

Summer would soon be upon us and time to begin planning for Head Start recruiting. Southeastern Vermont Community Action, a subsidiary of the United States Government, requested assistance in a need that arose in cooperation with the Rector of a local church, and a Head Start worker from a state College and a private Summer co-ed camp who would have a list of eligible local children and where to locate them. The parents were not too enthused about allowing their children to attend. They felt it was walking into the unknown because they were not notified of the program before-hand by the sponsors. A remedial reading teacher was hired for Head Start but the parents, especially the father of a family, refused to allow their child to attend, "because they learn quick enough at home." Some children were reluctantly allowed to attend. Head Start is a free pre-school program for children from low-income homes.

A low-income mother was hired as a paid employee but she needed a ride, ten miles, to and from work every day, being next to impossible to find. As a result, she could not accept the job. Most always, there was a car in the family, though it was usually used somewhere else when it was needed the most.

Contacts continued with the helping services for benefit of families; who at times refused to accept help. As in a case of a young man who was scheduled for referral to a mental health agency for evaluation, the parents refused, saying, "It isn't his fault that he's having problems in school." The father becoming adamant about allowing the evaluation, asking the very person attempting to assist to "leave us alone!"

What may have been a minor situation for the middle class could have become a stressful one for the disadvantaged in not having the use of a car. The parents loved their children and wanted the best for them even though someone else usually had to initiate an activity and provide the transportation. And living in a rural area, a car was a real necessity.

The 4-H projects were being very well accepted by the youngsters and their parents. When the projects were going full swing, members and leaders decided, with counseling from myself, a 4-H Achievement Day was in order so parents, friends and neighbors could see for themselves the activities in which the young people were involved. Plans were made for the presentation to be held at Bridgewater School. A news release was placed in the *Vermont Standard* weekly paper in the form of an invitation for the public to attend this first-ever Deer Run 4-H Club of Bridgewater Achievement Day.

Leaders and members were asked to present their project media to the best of their ability; after rehearsals. Members were given assignments as ushers, welcoming committee and what 4-H stands for. Each 4-H member explained their chosen project individually and what it has taught them. Parents and friends were very commendatory to the leaders for providing support for the youngsters and the know-how of hands-on work. The presentation was attended by Extension agent for youth, Ed Goodhouse, who expressed his appreciation to the leaders for taking an interest in the lives of the young people and to members for completing their projects.

Since I have already had the experience of visiting an abandoned gold mine, I asked the 4-H members if they would like to see what a mine looks like. They were ready to leave that very moment. I explained we must first ask permission of their parents. When permissions were granted, we picked a day in Spring and six young people and I were on our way. We drove up Baker Hill, leaving the car along the roadside to begin our not-too-short trek up the mountain, midst deciduous trees whose leaf buds were just beginning to open. Cedars, fir and pine of many varieties, red trillium, Dutchman's Breeches, Hepatica (Mayflower), Adder Tongues were well on their way to blooming in all their glory.

There are actually two different varieties of Dutchman's Breeches, or Boys and Girls, as they are sometimes called. One variety has a petal in the shape of boy's trousers reaching to the knees. Another variety actually has petals shaped similar to girl's frilly bloomers. The Adder Tongue is a yellow Spring flower resembling an Adder's tongue reaching out. Chickadees, Bluejays and the most beautiful of birds, the Cardinal, were calling to us as we trudged up the mountainside, each of us carrying a substantial stick, found on the ground, for support. We came upon cellar holes over which once stood houses, stone fences encircling dooryards and old apple orchards. All of this surrounded by under-growth; what at one time, centuries ago, was a working farm or homestead . . . where families lived and worked to eke out a living. When, in the distance, a huge pile of tailings appeared, they exclaimed in unison, "What's that??" I explained, "It is the material removed from the earth while digging, in order to reach the gold. When you see a pile such as this in the mountains, you will know that, somewhere very close, is an abandoned mine." Soon, amongst the under-growth, we could make out what appeared to be an opening into the earth. Approaching nearer, a wooden door frame came into view; from which hung a creaking, swinging door on a leather hinge. We stopped in our tracks. "Are we really here," they asked. "We have arrived," I announced. Water was dripping into the darkened mine; as we placed our sticks on a pile and made our way inside. A flashlight was a very necessary piece of equipment to have along as we were led by our desires across water puddles produced by the mountain springs, making very slushy walking. As the water dripped on our heads, rocks lined our path every-which-way causing us to place our feet surreptitiously, lest we slip into the puddles laying at our feet.

What better place than an open mine to hear our own voices reverberating through the mine. Someone asked, "Are there bear in these woods?" Before I could answer: LOOK! Bear tracks, almost under our feet! Luckily, headed to the outside. We've already walked at least one hundred feet and as I had the responsibility of looking after the youngsters, I decided it might just be the time to make our way back to the outdoors or have the unpleasant experience of coming in contact with the bear for which I was not prepared. We sloshed and slipped our way out; everyone talking and having fun as we reached daylight.

It was a wonderful place and time to enjoy the signs of Spring, unfolding flowers, budding trees, the sounds of the stream as it flowed inches from our feet. We all stop at once and listen to the sounds of silence all around us, then we fall to the ground to rest awhile.

The kids expressed their appreciation for being given the privilege of visiting what was, centuries ago, a real working gold mine. The trip taught the youngsters there was work involved in removing gold from the earth. Not just with machines but with their picks and bare hands as well. To actually touch the veins in the walls and explain to them it is actually gold they are touching and having the opportunity to walk in the footsteps of miners who struggled, centuries ago, to make a living for their families was a walk into history!

When we arrived at my home, the makings of a picnic were brought out: hot dogs, buns, pickles, potato salad, catsup, mustard and punch. The dogs were placed on each one's stick, found on the ground in my back yard; over a fire they were taught to build; inches away from a mountain stream and to put out when we were ready to leave the area. They all agreed this day turned out to be one of the best days of our lives!

RECIPE FOR A HAPPY VISTA VOLUNTEER

Take twelve full months of VISTA work; divide each of these months into twenty-eight, thirty or thirty-one parts. Prepare one part at a time as follows:

> Into each put <u>twelve</u> parts of work (some omit this ingredient and thus spoil the impression of the VISTA role), <u>eleven</u> parts of courage, <u>ten</u> parts of personality, <u>nine</u> parts of loyalty, <u>eight</u> parts of being able to understand the needs of others, <u>seven</u> parts of kindness, <u>six</u> parts of togetherness, <u>five</u> parts of getting to know you, <u>four</u> parts of responsibility, <u>three</u> parts of wisdom and perseverance, <u>two</u> parts of recreation (leaving this out is like leaving the trees out of the forest), and <u>one</u> part of frustrations and rewards.
>
> To this add a dash of fun, a sprinkle of play and a cupful of good humor. Pour into the whole mixture lots of leadership and love. Cook thoroughly with glowing and gentle warmth, garnish with miles of smiles and a sprig of everlasting joy. Serve with unselfishness and cheerfulness. Happy VISTAs are sure to result!
>
> And remember, the 'parts' are not necessarily in order of importance!
>
> Written by this VISTA Volunteer

PLEASE HEAR WHAT I'M NOT SAYING

Don't be fooled by me.

Don't be fooled by the face I wear. For I wear a mask, I wear a thousand masks.

And none of them are me.

I give you the impression that I am secure;

That all is sunny and unruffled with me; within as well as without.

That confidence is my name and coolness my game, that the waters are calm

and I'm in command and that I need no one.

But don't believe me, please!

My surface may <u>seem</u> smooth, but my surface is my mask.

Beneath dwells the <u>real</u> me . . . in confusion, in fear, in alone-ness.

But I hide this.

I don't want anybody to know it.

I panic at the thought of my weakness and fear being exposed.

That's why I frantically create a mask to hide behind.

To shield me from the glance that knows.

But such a glance is my salvation. My only salvation.

And I know it.

That is, if it's followed by <u>acceptance</u>, if it's followed by <u>love</u>.

It's the only thing that can liberate me . . . from myself.

From my own self-built prison walls.

From the barriers that I so painstakingly erect.

It's the only thing that will assure me of what I can't assure myself.

That I'm really worth something.

But I don't tell you this; I don't care, I'm afraid to.

I'm afraid your glance will not be followed by <u>acceptance</u> and <u>love</u>.

I'm afraid you'll think less of me, that you'll laugh.

And your laugh would kill me.

I'm afraid that deep down I'm nothing, that I'm just no good.

And that you will see this and you will reject me.

So I play my game, my desperate pretending game.

As a trembling child within.

I dislike hiding. Honestly.

I dislike the superficial game I'm playing.

I'd really like to be genuine and spontaneous . . . and me.

But you've got to help me.

You've got to hold out your hand.

Even when that's the last thing I seem to want . . . or need.

Only you can wipe away from my eyes the blank stare.

Each time you're kind and gentle and encouraging.

Each time you try to understand <u>because you really care</u>.

My heart begins to grow wings, very small wings, very feeble wings but <u>wings</u>.

With your <u>sensitivity</u> and <u>sympathy</u> and your <u>power of understanding</u>.

You can breathe life into me. I want you to know that.

I want you to know how important you are to me.

You can be a creator of the person that is me, if you choose to.

Please choose to.

You alone can break down the wall behind which I tremble.

You alone can remove my mask.

Do not pass me by.

<u>Please</u>, do not pass me by.

I fight against the very thing that I cry out for.

But I am told that <u>love</u> is stronger than strong walls and in this lies my hope. My only hope.

Please try to beat down those walls with firm, but gentle hands . . . and <u>caring</u>.

WHO AM I? You may wonder. I am someone you know very well.

For I am every man you meet and every woman you meet and every child you meet;

in your role as a VISTA Volunteer.

In this fight . . . in this War On Poverty.

I AM THE POOR!

    Written by a member of the community.

CHAPTER XIII

VERMONT'S BLACKBERRIES

"Whose woods these are . . . I think I know,
  His house is in the village, though.
  He will not see me standing there
    To watch his woods fill up with snow."

Robert Frost

When I first met Agnes, she looked like a woman eager to talk to this stranger who knocked on her door to ask for assistance in a project I was planning. Her face showed signs of much hard work; her hair salt and pepper gray, her home reflecting a kind of disarray that told me she may not have the time or strength to put things away.

Her family consisted of a husband and seven children plus a dog and several cats cavorting from tables to furniture. They lived in a house that clearly bore the test of time, situated on a busy State highway in a low valley with the foothills touching a fast-flowing stream across the road from their home . . . a beautiful area in the heart of the Green Mountains.

The kitchen floor had rough, wide floor boards, appearing clean enough 'to eat off of' covered here and there with worn throw rugs. Time-worn furniture lined the walls in the kitchen and living room. Running water was non-existent, a rainwater cistern with a handpump near the faucetless sink in a small kitchen alcove provided water for drinking, cooking and laundry . . . done by hand in a washtub. A two-holder stood behind the house. There was only minimum storage provided for kitchen utensils, so piles of pots and pans sat here and there in the kitchen wherever a space was found. The house was heated with a cast-iron wood cook stove in the kitchen and a round cast-iron 'parlor-type' wood stove in the living room. Five of the children were away on their own by then; the two younger children were at home and attending grade school.

I could not help but admire this woman, who raised their children and kept house midst inconveniences in a modern age; not twenty feet from the edge of the busy road. The home had two bedrooms on the ground floor and an unfinished attic (with a rough open ladder-type stairway) used for company. They kept abreast of the times with a small radio and an old television that 'didn't always work.' A work horse (kept for hauling wood) was housed in the three-stall barn, next to the house, along with a flock of chickens and ducks, a cow and two hogs.

Agnes said, "I take care of all the animals myself," as she showed me the barn and animals. There was hay to pitch for the horse and cow, barn cleaning, animal feeding and cow milking. Wood for the stoves was piled on the open-air front porch to make it easy to bring in the wood during heavy snow. With a sandy, front yard, there was no mowing to be done. Open cracks and holes in the walls near the floor were plugged with rags to keep out the cold, rodents and other small animals.

Agnes told me one day in Summer, "My four-year-old grandson told me he didn't want to come into my house anymore because he didn't want to see anymore snakes." Then, she explained it to me. It seems the dog became excited one day as he stood near one of the rag-stuffed holes, barking continuously. Attempts to quiet his barking were to no avail, so she decided to check it out. Suddenly, as she was peering near the opening in the wall, a three-foot-long spotted adder poked his head out and slithered into the room! She yelled for help but no one was around to hear. Not wanting to take her eyes off the creature, she had no choice but to leave the room to grab a broom from the kitchen. When she returned, the snake was nowhere in sight. What to do? She watched and waited and searched; said she, "I didn't know if I wanted to sleep in the house that night." Next morning, as she walked to the barn for her daily chores, she spotted it slithering through the weeds and tall grass near the barn. She said, "I grabbed a stick and took care of it, hoping it was the same one."

Her husband was proud of the fact that "this house stood long before we were married," though by then, badly in need of repair and maintenance. Many mountain people save on property taxes by not making improvements to their homes and as a result, they fall to ruin. Her husband was a true New Englander, living by the old adage, "use it up, wear it out, make it do or do without."

Words cannot describe the determination, courage and patience of this woman. Having to raise her children with traffic practically under her feet must have provided some anxious moments. Her husband is gone now and Agnes continues to live in the 'house by the side of the road.'

Vermont has many interesting incidents occurring as one travels the back roads. As the State is eighty percent forest, it is not unusual to come upon wild animals along the dirt roads in the back woods.

On a bright, May morning, I was driving on a country road attempting to locate a certain family. As I continued on, next to a dense, wooded area, a white-tailed deer came bounding out of the woods directly in front of my car. I quickly applied the brakes to avoid hitting him. Behind him came another and another. The first animal continued in a gallop across the road into an open field of clover; stopping in his tracks to gaze at the activity about to take place on the road. The second deer ran in front of my car, as I was stopped in the roadway and he remained there; staring at the gray monster with four wheels. The third deer also stopped. As I sat 'frozen' in my car waiting for the event about to take place, he began walking and sniffing all around the car and windows. As the deer went about his inquisitiveness, I began to get the feeling I was being invaded by aliens from outer space! The second deer decided to get into the act; coming closer to the car, checking out the headlights and windshield, walking around the perimeter of the car. I sat without moving a muscle; still waiting for the inevitable to happen: that something will frighten both animals and they will make a dash for safety across the top of my car. By then, my pulse was racing as I watched and waited to see exactly how they'll make their getaway. Just then I felt a sneeze coming on and in trying to subdue it, made a slight movement and in the quick getaway one of the deer jumped over the hood of the car. I watched in disbelief, surprised the windshield was still intact, as they dashed off into the field, joining the first one who was still standing in the same spot, not knowing what he was missing.

When driving after dark, returning from conferences or visiting families, a careful watch had to be in order for the deer alongside the roadways. Usually, they couldn't be mistaken with their glowing eyes readily seen unless they decided to make a quick dash across the road. In those instances, I breathed a sign of relief that once again, I made it through safely.

Natives said New England has five Seasons: Spring, Summer, Autumn, Winter and Mud. Mud Season could be anywhere when there is an abundance of glacial rock with no drainage to dry out the ground. Many drives took me into ravines where mud collected and snow remained until early Summer; making matters still worse for driving. I tried to stay clear of those places, even though at times it was a necessity to locate a family with a message perhaps or illness in the family. To make the going easier, I left the car along higher ground and walked the distance to the house. Steep mountain roads were as bad, especially in deep woods. Trying to find a spot to drive around the mud holes was next to impossible. Birch trees were prevalent, having a shallow root system; they begin to bend every which way and finally break or bend with their tops touching the ground over the dirt road. In those times, the only thing left to do was to get out of the car and remove the tree and/or branch. If that was not possible, my only alternative then, was to back down the steep grade of the mountain; hoping and praying all the while the brakes will hold.

Blackberrying was always my favorite past-time. So when Darlene asked me to accompany her into the blackberry patch, I accepted graciously. Everyone knows how to pick wild blackberries ... or do they? Blackberrying is not a pleasant little trip to the edge of the meadow with a pail swinging alongside; it is an encounter and a full-fledged battle. Along with a pail, one must arm oneself with clothing fit for an Eskimo ... an armor against evil spirits in the form of mosquitoes. A mosquito repellent might not only come in handy for a tour into the woods but can be a real necessity.

Considering blackberries become ripe in August, what, you may ask, are mosquitoes doing out in the heat of a Summer afternoon? It is true that these carnivorous beasts are most plentiful in the Spring, but enough remain to congregate in low areas and thickets. Not only are there mosquitoes in these beautiful berry patches, but an abundance of black flies which can take the fun out of an otherwise pleasant afternoon.

Don't try to go out in a short-sleeved shirt and shorts because you will never survive to tell about it! The uniform for berry picking consists of a pair of heavy blue jeans, a heavy shirt with a collar that can be turned up, heavy socks and sturdy ankle-high boots. A bandanna tied like an Aunt Jemima bonnet finishes off this striking ensemble. Gloves may come in handy to push away the brambles but are useless for picking the juicy fruit.

The first thing to do is to pick all the berries you can reach by skirting the thicket. This gives you half enough to do anything with, but also incentive enough to keep going. Now comes the hard part! Unless a berry-loving bear has already made a path through the brambles for you to follow, you will need to remove those prickly canes in order to get to the most beautiful berries that are always on the other side. By pulling a vine back and catching it on another (yes, even thorns have their uses), it gives you room to move on to the next thorny cane, which, as you are trying to disconnect it, has a habit of catching onto your bandanna; pulling it off to hang onto another thorny cane just out of reach; exposing your head to the beastly mosquito.

Many years ago, my Grandmother enjoyed telling the account of the day she gathered her tin pail (when homesteads were still almost one hundred percent forest; which meant a multitude of those juicy berries would be available) and headed out into the thicket, hoping to bring a heaping pailful of berries back home. It seems she always traveled alone on her walks into the woods. Even though the fruit was always available somewhere within sight of the trail, she would wander off deeper into the thicket.

On one particular day, as she strolled along with her pail half-full, happy, too, that she found so many in such a short time . . . she spotted a black bear making his way toward her, with his usual slow-moving, determined gait and moan. What did she do? She didn't hesitate for one minute because she knew a bear's favorite food is the blackberry and something had to be done; and quick! She placed her half-filled pail on the ground in front of her and took off in a sprightly manner in the opposite direction; never looking back, and never returning to that same spot again. Said she, "I never found out if my empty pail was still on the path waiting for me."

History almost repeated itself when Darlene and I took off from her home, clothed in armor against the black flies and beastly mosquitoes on our walk into the mountain behind her home to pick blackberries. It was a good mile walk up the dirt road that warm, August day when the berries were at their peak of ripeness . . . a looked-forward-to experience for me after establishing rapport with this lady who became my friend through her children. (She was the mother of the young man who refused to stay at 4-H camp and of the child who almost froze in the icy river.) She mentioned to me earlier in the week that, a few days before, as she hunted for berries alone, bear tracks were everywhere. She said, "I was hoping to get my pail filled before the bear saw me. Then, suddenly, I saw a movement in the tall bushes not far from where I stood. I knew it was a bear because of all the tracks around. I didn't wait for him to appear; I took off for home." We found the spot she spoke about, an area of thick, eight-foot tall (yes, eight feet tall) brambles separated in places by several feet where a very large animal apparently lumbered through and numerous bear tracks. We searched several places but berries were nowhere to be found; the bear having reached them before we did, no doubt.

Then Darlene asked me, "Rose, what would you do if you saw a bear?" She took me by surprise. At that moment, I was speechless. I wanted to see one but only in a convenient place; over on the next hill, perhaps, or from my car. Right now, seeing only tracks and the very large openings through the brambles was enough satisfaction for me. That alone was sufficient, for me to realize I should have respect for his size and his privacy and to leave well enough alone. We came home with empty pails!

CHAPTER XIV

I WAS A STRANGER

"It isn't what happens to you, but . . . how you handle it, that counts."

My VISTA service would be ending in a few days. I visited many families to bid them farewell; midst tears, and to check out several projects I would know will continue:
4-H, Geri-Teens, health education, young people's programs.

A young male VISTA arrived to take my place. And as I drove him around the community to acquaint him with the surroundings and meet some of the people he would be seeing, my memories took over and I found myself in his place; while attempting to find my own way around when I first arrived.

Before leaving my VISTA service in Bridgewater, I was asked again to take part in an interview during breakfast at Hanover Inn for a radio broadcast. An interesting affair, with members of the village council, business people, private citizens and helping organizations attending. Many questions were put forth; reasons for joining VISTA, where are the poor going now that you are leaving, what has been accomplished so far and the aspects of where the low-income stand in relationship to the middle-class.

Upon my return home, I began work at a local hospital; at the same time volunteering for local organizations. I was restless. A Catholic priest in Vermont told me, "Rose, you will never be happy working in a confined area of a hospital again." I didn't agree with him; considering the satisfaction I received from my nursing career before deciding on VISTA.

Before too many months went by, I began to realize how much his words were coming true for me; and I thought of them frequently as a hospital care-giver. I missed 'my people' whom I left behind. I missed familiar faces. I missed my 4-H kids. My thoughts reflected back on my VISTA work in Vermont. I could not get over my need to return working with the poor: their problems, their tears, their joys. Was it a call I began hearing again? Is it my destiny that I return to help the less privileged once again?

I contacted my former VISTA supervisor in Washington, D.C. He requested a resume of my work at my previous assignment in Bridgewater. I WAS ACCEPTED. Again to return to an area of my choice in the East. My heart soared as on eagle's wings!!

I chose an area near Bennington, Vermont; considering VISTA Washington was not placing volunteers in Central Vermont at that time.

Once again, I packed my bags for another year. On November tenth, nineteen hundred seventy, I arrived in Bennington, third largest city in the State of Vermont; situated at the southernmost corner of the State; a quaint village sitting a stone's throw from Mt. Anthony to the South and Bald Mountain to the East. It is also the home of the Bennington Monument, a three hundred six foot tall monolith, built in eighteen hundred one in commemoration of the attack launched from there by General Stark of the American Colonial Army against troops of General Burgoyne during the Revolutionary War. It is also the home of the renowned Bennington College, a private women's college then but now co-educational.

My immediate VISTA supervisor in Bennington was the director of the Bennington-Rutland Opportunity Council, or BROC, to which I was assigned. I would be driving my own auto with maintenance provided, I was told.

As VISTAs have the responsibility of finding their own living quarters when arriving at a VISTA site, I reserved a motel for two nights in the heart of the village, for the time being, with a 'bed of stone' I was not able to tolerate for more than the two nights!

Next morning, I visited BROC's office and introduced myself. The welcoming committee was great; that is, the office staff, but my new boss had other things on his mind; and couldn't be bothered, giving me the impression he didn't *need* or *want* any more help. "What's going on??" No immediate needs?? so much as to say, "We have enough VISTAs, we don't need you." A let-down, if there ever was one, and no one to listen to my problem!

Disappointment is a blasting experience, especially when high expectations are suddenly turned into denial and grief. The worst thing I could have done with it was weep; AND I DID! But, when I had a serious purpose in my life, tossing disappointment over my shoulder and hoping it would go away was not a solution. I had to handle it. And hard as it was to believe, these very feelings led to a really intense-type of happiness. Remembering the old adage: "people are about as happy as they make up their minds to be," the things that made up my disappointment proved to be the solid foundation upon which a truly satisfactory-type of life was built. Religious faith, hard work and a commitment to a worthy cause . . . all these were the beginning. And I have put them to work.

Catherine Whitman was a BROC Community Aide and knew of a lady who might rent a small apartment in her home for the time being. Daisy Myers was that gracious lady from whom I would be renting; though she would need to close her Summer home on the mountain and move into her town apartment when Winter closed in.

Located in the center of the village, close to low-income family homes and downtown businesses, it was where I hung my hat for the next three weeks. My contacts began with knocking on doors where families lived, visited business places, schools, newspaper offices and many administrative offices where I might receive information on the needs of the city and community. I decided to begin in the field of youth and Senior Citizens. I organized a hearing clinic for the Seniors at their request, listened to the problems of the poor and when I spoke with the High School Principal, he explained some of the special education classes and on-going physical education programs, already teaching First Aid. I inquired if he would be interested in setting up a Medical Self-Help Project into the Physical Education class. It would teach such lessons as what to do when a doctor is unavailable in a disaster period, how to purify water, emergency childbirth, improvising during a nuclear disaster, CPR, radioactive fallout and shelter, healthful living in emergencies; among others. Following many contacts with the American Red Cross, organizations and leaders of the community, the class was incorporated into the Program to begin with the next school term.

The day arrived when Daisy was ready to close her Summer home and move back into her apartment where I was now living. Again, I needed to find another place to 'hang my hat.' I contacted a Catholic priest for assistance. He just happened to know of a lady who might have a room in her home for me. I knocked on her door one evening and introduced myself, explaining my need in locating a place to live. The kind, gracious lady of seventy-five years young invited me into the living room of her cozy, white clapboard house. "Come in, come in, child," she said, "Come in out of the cold," offering me a cup of tea. It was another great welcome I received from those who cared, since arriving in this quaint, old town and just what my heart needed. We walked upstairs where she showed me a clean, tiny room, newly-decorated and pleasant. I would have kitchen privileges and said she, "Consider it your home, too." As it was late November and several inches of snow had already fallen, the only available parking space was across the street from her home in a muddy, city parking lot. As I would be working late some nights and returning home after dark, I decided against taking the room. Nevertheless, I kept in touch with this wonderful lady and have never forgotten her kindness to me; especially when this stranger who was the one needing help this time, knocked on her door and was treated like a queen: "I was a stranger and you took me in."

When Catherine became aware of my problem, she informed me she had an empty, second-floor apartment in her home and would I be interested. The rent was more than my allowance would handle but I had no choice but to accept at this time. I would be eating hot dogs for awhile!

It was a pleasant abode with lots of storage and room for my piles of paper work. I had a view of Mt. Anthony from my back porch that held a 'sometimes working' television and a table where I placed my twelve-inch, artificial Christmas tree surrounded by a wax Nativity display. Next door was a used-car lot which, incidentally, was the scene of a botched break-in one evening after dark. As I stood at the window of my darkened kitchen, I saw what appeared to be a shadowy figure in front of a car with its hood up. As I intently watched to get a closer look at the scene taking place in the unlit parking lot, I realized it was indeed someone attempting to break into the auto. I dashed into my bedroom to phone the police. While away from the window, making the call, the figure disappeared. It was several minutes before the police arrived; checked around the autos parked there and apparently finding nothing, drove away, never to return.

It was December and despite the neglect and non-support from my supervisor, my work was coming along as well as I could expect, until... history repeated itself when a letter arrived in the mail informing me VISTA Washington will cease sending living allowance checks to VISTAs in the field! "OH NO, NOT AGAIN!" The checks would not be available until possibly December thirtieth or January fifteenth. Congress didn't approve funding once again for the VISTA program. Did they expect VISTAs to live on the love we were receiving from the people we served? I survived in my Bridgewater assignment; I will survive somehow again. I chose this work for the poor and I will stay with my people once again. Though I was told I would be given allowance for driving my car when I first arrived, nothing has been received from my sponsor. Now that my allowance check will not be arriving on time, I could not drive my car. Christmas Day arrived and, after attending Mass at the Veteran's Home at six o'clock in the morning, walking through knee-deep snow for the trek there and back five blocks, I returned to my apartment with thoughts of Mom and my children. I missed our Christmas dinners together and with fifty cents left in my pocket, I could hardly buy enough food to cook myself a meal. I warmed up a can of chicken soup . . . thankful for the privilege of being here amongst the poor, who know, already, the pain of poverty. I didn't have the use of my car but I had two good legs to trudge through the snow this Day, to visit an elderly couple who may not have the joy of visitors on this day of Jesus's birth.

A partial check arrived on January fourth. Now, at least, I could buy gas and pay the rent. The remainder of the check arrived two weeks later. I could now continue my home visiting and work on the projects in progress.

Following contact with the American Red Cross, a Mother's Aid course was in the making and many positive problems solved for the low-income, with assist from the helping organizations. I found a short street in the village I didn't know existed; tucked between the alley and another short street, where lived a pregnant young lady with her parents. She needed help with her home situation. Her father didn't want her in their home; she was then referred to social services. I was now beginning to feel like a real VISTA again.

Though I may have felt as a real VISTA, I also felt, due to the negativeness of my boss, I had to work harder so that, maybe, in due time, he would accept me and respond accordingly; reminding me of the story of the gazelle and the lion, who must outrun each other in order to survive! I reported to him in person on my activities weekly, but no attempts were made to show interest in my work . . 'too busy' to talk about the projects I had organized.

Even then, I considered it a special privilege to be a VISTA Volunteer. Yes, I got tired and discouraged and met with resistance. Was it worth it? Returning to my home at night after a long day helping families, I came with the knowledge I may have made a contribution to one who may have needed me.

CHAPTER XV

**WHEN THE RIPPLES REACHED
ANOTHER SHORE...**

"What, giving again," I ask in dismay, "And must I keep giving and giving away?" "Oh no," said the angel, piercing me through. "Just give until God stops giving to you."

My VISTA work led me to the area schools and the Co-operative Extension Service of Bennington to locate young people from poor families. I was also in touch with VISTA Washington in regards to the biased attitude shown me by my boss. I was unhappy with the responses I received from the BROC office and requested another assignment; either to another area of New England or to my home State of Michigan to be nearer to Mom; who tactfully hinted in a letter she wished I lived closer; a co-incident: Was God putting words in her mouth that I should listen to?

In a few short weeks, a letter came from VISTA Washington Director that I was being transferred to Northeastern Michigan Community Action Agency, with offices in Alpena, Michigan (NEMCA). I accepted the transfer and was elated that Mom's wish was coming true and my initial disappointment was turning into a really intense type of happiness. Once again, I made my rounds to tell my people farewell. For the past four months, I came into contact with people and their lives in this quaint village I have come to love. The children were, again, the reason for the rapport I was privileged to establish with the poor families; new people to me again "the black poor and the Spanish poor; the white poor and the children of all the poor." True, I have been blessed with the comforts of life but the real source of my contentment lay not in those comforts but in my volunteer families with whom I had many precious moments. I was not only alive but I LIVED; through their tears and their laughter, their disappointments and their joys; and bringing me to my deepest feeling about leaving my VISTA service in Vermont to return to Michigan to be nearer my aged mother. I have been very close to her these many years of my life and she cared for me and protected me and now she needed me and it was my turn to take care of her. It is difficult to leave a place you care about and I was torn apart.

My new assignment to NEMCA, where my ripples will reach another shore, located on the Western shore of Lake Huron, served twelve counties and I was assigned to four of those counties, namely: Ogemaw, Arenac, Oscoda and Iosco, of which West Branch, in Ogemaw County, pop. eight hundred, would be the core of my activities along with Harrison, Mio and Tawas.

A Community Action's purpose is to assist communities in analyzing their needs, assessing the resources available, and developing effective community programs to attack their poverty problems. Some of the programs under NEMCA's guidance were low-income housing, emergency food, Head Start, food stamps, Neighborhood Youth Corps, Family Planning, VISTA, Migrants, Foster Grandparents, and Outreach Workers. My assignment was to establish programs in health education and training, daycare, young people's groups, and general assistance to those in need, regardless of what the need may have been.

The Director of NEMCA was Bob Peters, my immediate supervisor being Pat Schaffer, whose headquarters was in Mio, a mostly-rural area twenty miles north of West Branch. It was there I met a pleasant lady, Elinor Killackey, an Outreach worker, who welcomed me with open arms and invited me to stay at their home until I found a permanent place to live. She and her husband, Ed, had a comfortable home in Rose City, eight miles north from her job in West Branch.

I welcomed the opportunity to have a place to stay and not have to hunt through that strange community about which I knew so little. Next day, I met my new boss, Bob; receiving my assignment and his expectations of my duties. Finding my way around the new rural area was not difficult, especially when Elinor and Ed were very generous with their time as soon as I stepped through their doorway; informing me of different work situations, showing me around their neighborhood and giving me the particulars of the counties where I would be serving.

Within a week's time my inservice training took place in Gaylord, Michigan, where I would meet many people with whom I would have contact in my new job with the poor. As were the initial contacts in my former VISTA assignments, I attempted to locate individuals who could give me information on the needs of the community.

VISTAs are expected to be on call twenty-four hours a day, seven days a week, in any sort of weather. I knew how changeable the weather can be, so frequent snowstorms in March soon after I arrived didn't stop me in my travels. The snowstorms continued into April, a most difficult time of year for driving throughout the countryside with mud season just around the corner; yes, Michigan has mud season, too. I made my way onto the back roads of the counties searching for the homes with families who have been referred to me through various agencies. Trees and branches leaned over roads in the hills and valleys. White-tailed deer were as plentiful here as they are in the East, where I could see herds grazing in open meadows.

Klacking Creek is a small community of historic homes interspersed with new homes where lived many of the people with whom I had been in contact. Young families, new mothers and pregnant girls were all on my 'help list.'

I met with Rev. James Suchoski, Pastor of St. Joseph parish in West Branch, to obtain knowledge about St. Joseph's Elementary School. The nuns and lay teachers were very kind in welcoming me to the community and to work out a day to meet with them for Glad Days, an annual affair similar to a Summer Camp for youngsters, ages seven through twelve, and held on the church grounds.

One day, Elinor made me aware of a cabin for rent on the banks of the Rifle River in the small community of Churchill, eight miles from West Branch, consisting of a Post Office, mechanic's garage, general country store (carrying everything from milk to mouse traps), several homes; some historic, some new; homes of the elderly and young alike. The general store was owned and run by Claude and Lenora Webster who also owned the rental cabin. When I visited them to inquire about renting the cabin, they knew about VISTA Volunteers as one had already arrived some months ago but were not familiar with the work we did. They were quick to explain, the cabin had no running water nor an indoor toilet. Lenora said, "You will need to carry water from the faucet located out on our back porch (a hundred feet from the cabin) and use the outdoor toilet just up the hill." I asked to see the interior of the cabin before I decided if it was what I was looking for. As she unlocked the only door leading to the one-room cabin, I knew I wanted it, reminding me of the one I left in Bridgewater Center, Vermont.

It was a small, square, white wood-sided building with an electric range, refrigerator, faucet-less sink, two double beds separated by a wall of wood and curtains for privacy. A sofa bed, wooden table and chairs furnished the living area; heated by a radiant oil-burning heater and surrounded by windows on all four sides. A charming and cozy abode. There was ample parking in front, facing the beautiful, fast-flowing Rifle River. "I'll take it," I told her. The monthly rent was reasonable enough to go with my living allowance. I moved in the next day.

As Spring and Summer arrived, many canoeists were using the river for recreation. A Blue Heron, who frequently stood in the middle of the river for long periods of time, knew it wasn't such a bad place to catch fish. The white-tailed deer were seen at daybreak taking in the cool, river water and at night feasting on the apples just outside my cabin windows.

The more canoeists using the river, the more would be using my two-holer. The yard was very large between the road and my cabin where the grass was regularly mowed but left to grow tall in a certain low area. Snakes were plentiful near the river and my cabin; in fact, I was not sure whether one of them might be lying-in-wait for me whenever I opened the door to the outhouse . . . ever so slowly! That, thank you, has never happened, but . . . when I saw two girls come out of a canoe and head straight for the outhouse right through the tall grass, I waited in awe to see what was about to happen. Suddenly, one of the girls let out an earth-shattering scream as soon as she stepped into the low-lying area. Her friend yelled out to her,

"What's the matter with you?" She screamed back to her friend, "Stay out of there, there's a snake in the grass."

On a warm weekend day, as I was washing my car in the driveway, hauling water from the river by buckets-full, I had my tank cleaner outdoors with the electric cord lying on the ground. Finishing the exterior cleaning, I started to reach toward the ground to pick up the cord. I pulled my hand away quicker than I could say, "DON'T" . . . a snake was moving along the cord, possibly thinking it was another of his own kind!

The Red Cross staff was planning a Mother's Aide course and needed help with recruiting young people for the class. It was to teach baby sitting in all its aspects from newborns to five year olds. Most mothers were receptive to the idea and a class came into being. Held in the Rose City Elementary School, the class, sponsored by the American Red Cross and VISTA, taught twelve to fourteen-year-olds the values of good nutrition, emergency and safety measures, child growth and development, recreation and discipline, handling the small baby, bathing, feeding, proper use of the phone, what to do when the doorbell rings when the parents are away, good grooming ideas, First Aid, and the responsibility while baby-sitting. It was taught by Red Cross personnel, mothers, nurses of the community and a doctor spoke on the subject of when to call the doctor. An eight-week course, members received American Red Cross certificates qualifying them as trained baby sitters, many getting jobs during Summer vacation. As many of the participants were 4-H members, it counted as a summer 4-H project.

In my travels, I found several young women needing guidance in their pregnancies. With support from the District Health Department of West Branch, a pre-natal class was formed after much searching and recruiting interested women. Instructors were provided by the health department. A doctor talked on all aspects of pregnancy and childbirth. Following the six-week class, presented free of charge, a tour of the Tolfree Memorial Hospital was arranged with the hospital administrator explaining first-hand the surroundings to which the mothers-to-be will be exposed before, during and after delivery.

Contacts with regional leaders continued, much rapport being established with many families and organizations, making it less difficult to carry on with what I had planned.

While all the various classes were going on, a need arose for the public to be made aware of the techniques of oral resuscitation (mouth-to-mouth) or C.P.R. A State Police trooper of West Branch presented the demonstration, given on Resusci-Annie for the benefit of Ogemaw Heights School System and the general public. Held at the high school, many people learned the value of knowing how to assist an individual in cases of choking and/or reviving someone who stopped breathing, whether an adult or a child.

A teaching nun from St. Joseph Catholic School requested I join their Senior High Family Living group as a class to discuss my work with the poor and furnish information on becoming a VISTA Volunteer. I prepared a format on how to go about general household duties, approaching people with problems, problem solving and why I became a VISTA. They were certainly an interesting audience and a far cry from what I had been familiar with during my training and placement, namely: reaching out to the poor. The four-day session made me realize these young people will succeed in life; they were well-mannered, interested in their specific communities and concerned about their own lives; even wanting to learn how to go about joining VISTA, which surprised their teacher.

Mother's Day would soon be upon us and the Klacking Creek Holy Family Society asked me to be their principal speaker at their Mother-Daughter banquet, speaking on the role of motherhood and my VISTA work in their community.

Before I could take another breather, the Senior Citizens of Skidway Lake contacted me in regards to presenting a health-screening clinic in their tiny community. The health department took the responsibility of obtaining volunteer workers for blood-pressure readings, blood glucose (diabetes testing), tuberculin skin testing (for TB) and tonometry (glaucoma testing). It was set up for the general public over thirty years of age. Held in the Skidway Lake Township Hall, over one hundred eighty people were screened, with several found having elevated blood sugar and blood pressure while a few tested positive for tuberculosis.

This was a pilot program and if successful, another would be planned for the near future. As a clinic such as this could not be successful without much publicity, I worked hard to promote the importance of a clinic of this order. As a result, due to the large number of interested citizens participating, it was decided to hold another within a few months.

The demand as a speaker was growing; telling and re-telling the processes of the VISTA Volunteer, my purpose in the communities and projects on-going. As much as the VISTA organization was publicized, so many residents and business people were unaware of the activities we organize and for what the program really stood. It was good to talk to and with them about my work and the needs of communities and unseen poverty one encounters, once one steps off the beaten path. People were most considerate and empathic in regards to my work and offered monetary assistance for various projects requiring funds for continued involvement.

In July, the Co-operative Extension Service sponsored a week-long 4-H camp at Camp Grayling, a National Army Reserve Headquarters, fifty miles north in Oscoda County. The Ogemaw County agent for youth, Jerry Malosh, asked me to volunteer as one of the camp nurses, giving me the opportunity to work with young people again.

The temperature was ninety degrees when I left my home that hot, July afternoon. Halfway to camp the radiator on my nineteen sixty-six Buick Wagon blew. I pulled off the road and waited for the engine to cool before continuing my journey. By now, I had another thirty miles to travel. Stopping at a farm house for assistance, I was able to get a bucket of water to take along, just in case. Two more radiator blowouts occurred and three hours later I drove into camp, registered, and shown my health clinic. A jumble of kids were running around, trying to find their places. Evening brought more 4-H'ers dashing to and fro, as we prepared for a hot dog roast and community singing, while a multitude of beastly mosquitoes attempted to take over.

Helen was the camp nurse supervisor. 'OH NO, is *this* what we'll have to put up with tonight? By now, the flying monsters found a comfortable place to spend the night . . . right above our camp cots! It was a hot, steamy night. We covered our heads with our top sheet while we fought to breathe but the attack army stung right through the material.

Campers were coming in with their ills: nausea, sore throats, bug bites and skin rashes, to name a few. Days were filled with hikes in the woods nearby, baseball games, water sports, learning projects, arts and crafts and hands-on activities and outdoor cookouts. Following a week of ills and homesickness for the campers; frustrations, lack of sleep and bug bites for the nurses, we were all ready to return to the comforts of our homes.

Since transferring to Michigan on my VISTA assignment, I had the opportunity and privilege of seeing Mom more frequently. I tried to visit her every two weeks at her home in Traverse City, one hundred miles from my work area. It was a wonderful way of realizing what an intense type of happiness God has given to me and to my Mom. She was happier now that she knew her wish has been granted and I lived closer to her.

On a mostly sunny, Sunday afternoon in summer, returning to my work site in Ogemaw County after spending the weekend with Mom, I took a different road . . . a road not taken before that time. As I drove on, having approximately fifty miles to travel yet, dark clouds began appearing on the horizon, while the sun was attempting to win out and continued to shine. Soon, the sun disappeared and I saw a lightning flash and heard a thunder-clap with several raindrops splashed onto the windshield of my car. "Oh, oh, will I be driving in a rainstorm or will it be a gentle rain accompanying me on my journey. It *is* a much-needed rain," I said to myself.

The air was beginning to smell clean and pure and dust being washed off every leaf and flower. Along with the rain, the sun came out, making everything brighter. We know it takes both sun and rain to bring the extraordinary magic of a rainbow. I began to sing: "Somewhere *over* the rainbow, skies are blue and the dreams that we dare to dream really do come true. Somewhere *over* the rainbow, bluebirds fly; birds fly over the rainbow, why, then, oh, why can't I?" Beautiful words!

Traveling East on a straight, lightly-traveled secondary road, as the rain continued to fall and the sun played peek-a-boo with the rain clouds, a rainbow began to appear in the distance. I watched it as I drove along on that long, straight highway and was surprised it was getting brighter and not losing its beautiful rainbow colors. I could not keep my eyes off it and noticed I was getting nearer and nearer to it. Then, I saw it; a long, colorful arc beginning at one side of a field, reaching across the road in front of me ending at the edge of a woods on the other side. IT TOOK MY BREATH AWAY! I slowed my car almost to a stand-still . . . this huge colorful arc right in front of me! I sat enchanted by the beautiful spectrum of colors for a long moment. Then, I began driving my car ever so slowly closer to the colorful arc and knew what was about to happen . . . I found myself driving precisely *under* the rainbow! Sending shivers up my spine, I had to pull off the road to gather my senses and try to believe, for myself, what had taken place. It was not a mirage and I had to admit to myself 'I really did travel *under* a rainbow' as I could not see it anymore because I left it behind.

Like the bluebirds flying *over* a rainbow, my dreams will come true by driving *under* it!

CHAPTER XVI

THE LAST FAREWELL

"There are plateaus to achievement in everyone's life . . . pauses when we can stop, briefly, to re-assess our progress. But there is no end to what anyone can accomplish."

In the midst of my activities when I felt a need for some rest and relaxation, I took my week's vacation to the White Mountains of New Hampshire, the Green Mountains of Vermont, Historic Boston and the Maine Coast. My son, Tom, Mom, and grandson Brian, age six, came along for the trip. It was an experience having a six-year-old along who was a tree climber and a monster-man behind the boulders of the state parks, where we slept in the lean-tos; three-sided buildings with a sloping roof in the back; cooking our breakfasts on the open grill provided. We visited Lost River cave and Polar Caves and where we squeezed our bodies through the 'Orange Crush' and 'Lemon Squeezer' between the rocks of the caves, inches away from rushing water in a pitch-black space. Eons ago, prospectors from Canada hid their gold and cattle in these caves; illegally brought to America; through which we were now tracing their footsteps on hands and knees! The week was gone before we even thought about returning home.

My energy renewed, I accepted an invitation to serve as one of the counselors on an Ogemaw County 4-H exchange trip to Gallatin, Tennessee, with permission from my NEMCA supervisor. The group left one Sunday morning in July in a school bus and private auto, consisting of thirteen and fourteen-year-old girls and boys, numbering fifteen, along with six women and men counselors.

We arrived at a 4-H camp in Kentucky at eight o'clock in the evening; everyone ready for some stretching exercises following the day-long trip. We stayed overnight in an auditorium furnished with cots and using the sleeping bags we brought along. After enjoying an evening snack, we tried to sleep midst flying insects and countless groups arriving and leaving.

Morning found agents, leaders and 4-H'ers cooking breakfast outdoors on the grills before leaving on the last leg of the trip. On the trip to Gallatin, we stopped at Mammoth Cave and a horse ranch near Millersburg, Kentucky, a beautiful place resembling a motel with many flowering plants in their containers gracefully hanging from the eaves of the horse barns. Mammoth Cave, if stretched out, would extend at least one hundred miles; or more than the distance from Philadelphia, Pennsylvania, to Washington, D.C. It is one of the world's largest and most majestic caverns, opening under a hillside in Southern

Kentucky. It has two hundred twenty-five avenues winding over five levels and a circumference of twelve miles.

One of the two access tunnels is wide enough to accommodate an interstate highway. Drops of steady, non-stop water have carved in the limestone floor twenty-three seemingly bottomless pits. One formation so closely resembles a waterfall it is named "Frozen Niagara." At seventy-five by forty-five feet, it is probably older than the real Niagara Falls. There are rooms as large as a basketball court; minutes later you're walking on a narrow ledge looking into deep gorges. Mammoth's history dates from seventeen ninety-eight, where guides feel good about their responsibility; that their sons can have no greater ambition than to 'guide the cave.'

Typical was a thirty-seven year old third-generation guide, born only a stone's throw across the hollow from the cave's entrance. He went away to college and taught Junior High School. But he couldn't get caving out of his system and returned to be a guide. "No matter how many times I walk through," he said, "Mammoth Cave fascinates me just as much as it did the first time." It is the lure of this fabulous under-ground cathedral.

Arriving in Gallatin at four o'clock in the afternoon, we were given a rousing welcome from the Tennessee 4-H'ers, their parents, agents and leaders, who had a meal spread out in a gymnasium on long tables, with food fit for kings and queens! Introduction games were played, tributes passed out to Extension agents and leaders and new friends made. The Gallatin 4-H'ers pulled up a chair directly in front of each one of their guests as we sat next to the gym wall and that's how friendships began.

After the meal, we left to make our abode with our host families for a week. My 'family' was Mr. and Mrs. William Watson of Portland, Tennessee; a gracious family, having a son in college and 4-H daughter in high school. Breakfasts with the Watsons were meals to remember; consisting of hot cakes, bacon, Southern-friend potatoes and fried tomatoes, a specialty in the South.

I had a comfortable room upstairs with a fan that proved to be a real necessity every night. The Southern heat was almost too much to bear. There were times when sleep didn't come until early morning, when it was time to greet another day. The cicadas sang in the twilight and tree toads kept me awake with their welcoming song and I loved it. (Cicadas are large fly-like insects with transparent wings.)

The day following our arrival, the entire Michigan-Tennessee group hopped on a bus to visit Johnny Cash's recording studio; all of us receiving a thrill when June Carter came out to greet us. On another day, we visited the steam plant of Gallatin, Fairview House, Hog Parlor and the Towns of #One and New Deal. The Hermitage and Andrew Jackson's birthplace was on another day's agenda. Tennessee 4-H camp, Columbia Country Music Hall of Fame, State Capitol and Museum were other places of interest along with being guests of the Noon television show in Nashville. To watch the beautiful horses prance through their paces at the Mama-Say-No-Farm was a delight indeed.

Our final day was spent on a picnic in a park, provided by the Tennessee 4-H group and County agents. While the adults sat at tables enjoying scrumptious food and good conversation; some of the young people mingled around and under the grand old oak trees standing near a fast-flowing stream. Suddenly, we heard a scream from one of the girls, "Get me out of here, there's a snake in the tree!" The kids scattered every which way toward the tables at which we sat, causing the rest of us to be extra cautious where we walked. On the tree, wrapped partially around a branch, was the four foot snake, appearing to prepare to drop down on someone's head!

The last night of our visit was reserved for a trip to the Grand Ol' Opry in Nashville (located in the downtown district then); a large auditorium with high bleachers on three sides. Supplying every guest with a cardboard fan (at a cost) as we entered, was an experience just seeing every fan moving rhythmically over the faces of the audience in that non-air conditioned place. A thrill it was, indeed, to watch the performers go through their acts with a que to the audience as to the exact time to applaud.

It was truly a memorable week for everyone and the Michigan 4-H'ers came back home with a feeling of contentment and appreciation for the great hospitality shown them while guests of a great organization, the 4-H Club of Gallatin, Tennessee.

The snowmobile group of West Branch was going strong but lacked a knowledge of First Aid as a required assignment. As director of the group, Jerry Malosh, Ogemaw County agent for youth asked me to present a class in First Aid. Preparing a format consisting of general directions for First Aid, the young men learned directions in moving the injured, sterilization of equipment, fractures, splints, cuts and bruises, bleeding, dislocations, shock and CPR. The bandage practice was most humor-provoking for the members as they attempted their bandaging techniques on each other.

The VISTA Volunteer program was now well known throughout several counties. The *Bay City Times*, a publication from Bay City, Michigan, ran a story about my work and presence in the area; with photos and VISTA information. The Mio Senior Citizens wanted to hear about my involvement and invited me to speak to them. It was an interesting group who were impressed with the workings of a VISTA Volunteer as they stated, "We didn't know anything like this even existed."

It was nearing Fall and 4-H leader banquets were in full swing and the colors of Autumn were beginning to appear in all their splendor and realizing the time was almost here when I must end my present year of VISTA service, I wanted to shout, "I'M COMING HOME, I'M COMING HOME" . . . But, how can I stand it when the tears flow at the very thought of leaving them . . . these wonderful people for whom I've done so little, but who have done so much for me!

My projects continued until the day came for me to leave. Many residents were inquiring about a Crisis Line for emergency cases. A meeting was arranged for interested individuals. It was November and many were gong to require financial assistance with heat and electricity. Many low-income and elderly were without phones; crime was on the rise in many secluded areas and they were afraid. "A crisis line would be helpful," the residents were telling us. Many get-togethers were held to begin the process of organization. The Ogemaw Heights High School Principal was interested in working on a referral line. So many individuals volunteered their services; helping to make it a reality.

The Fifty-Plus Club of Skidway Lake invited me to be their guest at Thanksgiving dinner in their Town Hall. They also extended their interest in the Crisis Line. It was good to know that this stranger who arrived in their midst, not so long ago, has been given the privilege to 'break bread' with them on a Holiday. And it mattered to me that I should accept their cordial invitation.

Before my departure, the Nuns of St. Joseph Convent invited me to dinner; a privilege indeed. We became good friends by my frequent visits and by their counseling these past eight months. But, they could not conceive in their minds how anyone could live in a humble cabin without running water and a two-holer and snakes as frequent visitors.

Citizens were telling me they wished someone would take care of the many junk cars spread across the countryside. "But how?" they said. Community leaders became interested; mechanics wanted to know what they could do. I sent for literature from one of the big auto makers in Detroit. They were very receptive to the idea and I received helpful information on how to begin the project. A meeting was held in regards to a junk car removal project. The idea spread and soon many people were working on it.

A week before my departure, I was asked to participate in a seminar at the Wurtsmith Air Force Base in Oscoda, Michigan, in regards to my three-year commitment to VISTA. The personnel were interested to hear the reasons why I have given those years of my life to being a Volunteer; and wanting to know the response from the low-income with whom I shared a part of my life.

The Crisis Line became a reality as my VISTA service with the Northeastern Michigan Commmunity Action Agency came to a close. Before leaving, many people who became my friends since arriving in the West Branch-Rose City-Tawas-Mio area, had a surprise luncheon for me at the West Branch Country Club; a beautiful affair with church leaders, newspapermen, helping organization's workers, business people, NEMCA staff, my immediate supervisor, Pat Schaffer, Extension Service staff and many friends came to bid me farewell. Forty in all . . . a tear-jerker for me if there ever was one, presenting me with a Holy Bible and many gifts for their appreciation.

CHAPTER XVII

SOME PATHS ARE MADE TO BE TAKEN ---
I HEARD A CALL . . . AND I ANSWERED IT!

God's work <u>must</u> truly be our own.

The War on Poverty started with individuals; a man, a woman, a child . . . taking them one by one. Poverty is need. It is lack of opportunity. It is helplessness to cope with hostile or uncaring institutions. It is lack of dignity.

The treatment the poor received at the hands of bureaucrats, at the hands of private industry, at the hands of landlords, is more than the poor should have had to endure. Poverty is a terrifying, impersonal and dehumanizing condition imposed on millions of Americans. Poverty is taking your children to the doctor's office and spending several hours waiting, with no one even taking your name; and coming back the next day and the next until they finally get around to you. Poverty is having a landlady who turns off the heat when she leaves for work in the morning and turns it back on when she returns at six o'clock in the evening. It's being helpless to do anything about it because by the time the officials get around to it, she has turned the heat back on for the night. Poverty is having a child with glaucoma and watching that eye condition grow worse day by day while the officials send you to the private agencies and they send you back to the welfare office and when you ask the officials to refer you to this special hospital they say they can't because you are of a different culture. They finally refer you, BUT IT IS TOO LATE!

Most Americans knew there were poor people but had no real knowledge of their lives or problems. Today, we know poverty still exists. We know there are elderly people who cannot purchase medicine due to limited incomes. We know children who have not eaten cannot learn. We know welfare recipients can and will work but there are no jobs for the under-educated. We know substandard housing is a health hazard. More importantly, we are aware poverty is not created by the poor but by imperfect systems failing to protect the haves and have-nots equally. We must be aware we *can* make a difference.

The many VISTA Volunteers working in the poverty programs have made a real contribution to this Country; entering invisible communities and working with invisible people. VISTAs have been aware that low-income citizens have few resources other than themselves. They made a tremendous impact on the lives of the poor by working to build the poor's confidence in their ability to help themselves. Because a VISTA cared, many of the poor assumed local leadership positions and learned to take advantage of resources they may have thought unavailable or rightfully theirs. VISTAs couldn't stop poverty by itself. We needed the work of every citizen of these United States to come forth and join the ranks of those who cared enough to sacrifice their time in the communities of the poor.

The work for the poor is far from over. To eliminate poverty, we must all join hands together because if we are not part of the solution, then we are part of the problem. Living in a state of continuous disadvantage, and in some cases several generations, the poor did not have an opportunity to learn of the help available to develop social, educational and economic skills. They were frustrated, from where many family problems arose. There were not many steady jobs available, especially for men. When they did work, they knew it would not be long before they were looking for another job. This, then, was a constant threat to their economic security.

Another factor placing the father at a disadvantage and leading to family difficulties was being aware it was much easier for women to get steady employment. It placed men in an insecure position; a feeling of inferiority. The role of breadwinner was taken from them. Life lived under these conditions demanded little verbal communication. Speech became crude. Children and spouses were abused. Men left their homes because they could not tolerate their feelings of worthlessness. Lack of motivation, hope and incentive is no less a powerful barrier than a lack of financial means. Thus, the cruel legacy of poverty is passed from parents to children. Poverty breeds poverty. A poor individual or family has a high probability of staying poor.

Low incomes carry with then risks of illness, immobility and limited access to education and training. Poor families cannot give their children opportunities for better health and education, needed to improve their lives.

Hunger is not which we associate with dinner being late or with periodic attempts to diet. Hunger is a gnawing pain, felt every day of their lives; families and children. Hunger is worry and anxiety because it means a persistent search for food. Hunger is grief; as mothers and fathers watch their children go without food. Hunger is humiliation, searching in litter bins. Hunger is fear of the future with its unknowns. Amongst all the under-privileged is birth and death, love and heartbreak, courage and despair, work and play, struggle and joy.

VISTA was the last great adventure available to Americans over eighteen years of age to serve in America ... the chance to enter into the hearts and minds and souls and feelings of a people, regardless of culture; a hard-earned disclosure but well worth it. Many young people who volunteered to work for VISTA say they favored extreme change of the social structure by their year of working with the poor. Almost no one talked in terms of dropping out or of violent demonstrations. The volunteers had more faith in their ability to bring about changes and more confidence in the integrity of the poor and the poor's desire to improve themselves. Said a former associate of O.E.O., "Out there in the ghettos and Indian Reservations they learned; for the first time how poor the poor really were. The kids wanted to get to the root of the problems.

They learned social change was a long and complicated business. Many were going back to school for careers in social work, teaching, community organizations and even law and politics following their year's commitment to VISTA."

One of the amazing things about being a VISTA was that I could go days without realizing I was a VISTA at all. I awakened mornings to the sound of roosters crowing at a nearby farm, the sounds of the rushing Ottauquechee River across the road, and the whisper of the wind in the mountain across the field of red clover, and I would think, amazed and unbelieving: "I'm in Vermont! Am I really a VISTA?" Just another person amongst the poor, working out my own problems and frustrations; like one more citizen of the State of Vermont. Even though each volunteer made his or her own story, the basic problems of poverty, fate and hunger were pretty much the same. VISTA existed as the great challenge for individual Americans. We didn't start with programs; we started with people. We knew the programs would follow. But those volunteers who sat back waiting for the world to come to them, might have had a totally different view of their year's work with the underprivileged. We needed to evaluate ourselves before going out into the field to work with people who would profit with a little love and attention. We had to make self-changes in our attitudes.

During training, our skills were being refined to adapt to the type of assignment we would eventually receive. It was a very real necessity to prepare ourselves for the understanding about living with people in poverty, the knowledge of the 'whys and hows' of poverty and an insight into the role of the area where we would be finally assigned. There had to be a confidence we would need to prepare us for the service that lay ahead. One can only scratch the surface in a year of volunteer work. Those who joined gained as much as they gave. They gained knowledge of the world they lived in and the confidence they could do something to improve it.

My three years of service to America as a VISTA was a unique experience . . . a memory that will remain with me for the remainder of my life. It was an opportunity for concerned persons to express their compassion for others in the most objective way, by contributing their most precious possession . . . their time; a year or years of their lives to the cause of improving the lives of others less fortunate. It was an adventure being in those strange places far from my family. Many times, feeling lonely and homesick, I would seek solace at one of the gentle streams flowing along the back roads in the Ogemaw Hills and the Green Mountains. It was hard to say good-bye to my family and friends. I wouldn't be seeing them for a long time, but to go to a place I knew nothing about and to share a part of my life and walk a mile in the shoes of those less privileged than I, was one of my greatest blessings.

I believe God has given every woman and every man, rich or poor, married or single, loaded with problems or joyfully carefree; at least one talent for serving. It doesn't have to be a big talent, just some one special thing; some small corner of yourself which is uniquely 'you.' If we examine ourselves carefully and ask God . . . in that naked and honest way, to guide us, surely we can discover some areas in which we can be used.

This assignment with VISTA responded to a definite need in the Bridgewater, Ogemaw and Oscoda communities, promoting what otherwise by themselves, the underprivileged, could not accomplish. We had to begin where the need was and gradually incorporate it into other areas of service. There's a tendency, when one feels nothing concrete was produced, to convince ourselves that nothing was accomplished. We cannot allow that belief to take away the truth of what happened there.

There is nothing imaginary or fictitious about these stories I have written. They describe the lives of people who live in parts of America that are not very well defined by the rest of society. What makes it even more troubling and risky for the poor, is they stand next to a very steep slope, having no assets or savings, no health insurance, no support. The solution to the welfare problem may be a mix of job training, remedial educational accessibility, real employment increases, child care so mothers can work and not have to spend all their money paying for that child care, some genuine health care and, of course, many other solutions no one has yet thought about.

Americans have not thought seriously about the problems of poverty since the days of the Great Depression. Even then, it took a long time for America to acknowledge that we were in serious trouble and ought to do something about it. In these past thirty years, we have begun to recognize that the richest Country in the world has its own poor. That, besides luxury, material abundance, affluence and extravagance; there is also poverty close by. Most people don't often think about the poor, who are often set off by themselves in the great urban centers or on rural back roads. We have done everything possible to render them invisible; who more often than not see the slums in our own front parlors, safely removed from contact by the TV tube.

Our Country doesn't always understand its own function when it sets out merely to give aid to the poor, to feed the hungry, to relieve the suffering. Even though these works of mercy must be done, they are only a Band-Aid approach. The task before America is to get rid of poverty. This may sound like an unrealistic dream that never will be or never *can* be. There are enough people who care in this vast Country of ours; people who care enough to make drastic changes in our society. We do not know what lies ahead but we are workers in the field and know what must be done and done quickly and faithfully.

We have enough study behind us to make a good beginning, enough planning to point the way to action. Of course, we do not know *all* that must be done in the years ahead but let us learn as we work; let us learn by doing.

In the nineteen sixties, then-President Lyndon B. Johnson said, "Eliminate poverty in the midst of plenty by opening to everyone the opportunity to work and the opportunity to live in decency and dignity." In the nineteen nineties, President William J. Clinton said, "The VISTA concept was straightforward. Its goal was great social advancements. It began its work in what we now see as the obvious place: in communities where the need was the greatest. VISTA taught us the importance and power of people building from within." These were the words taken from a publication I received as a VISTA Alumnae, announcing President Clinton's new National Service initiative, AmeriCorps*VISTA, swearing-in about fifteen thousand volunteers on the South Lawn of the White House in the Fall of nineteen ninety-four. In return for a one or two year commitment, participants will receive a living allowance upwards of seven thousand dollars a year. They'll receive health care and child care when needed. Volunteers will also receive an award of nine thousand four hundred fifty dollars to help pay for college or to repay student loans.

AmeriCorps*VISTA is the President's new program to absorb the talents, energy and experience of Americans from all walks of life. As with VISTA, AmeriCorps*VISTA is offering a helping hand in guidance and support to a generation of young and not-so-young Americans determined to prove themselves worthy of wanting to 'get things done' . . . a tradition on which VISTA was founded in nineteen sixty-four and on which AmeriCorps*VISTA will continue to build.

Readers of this book interested in learning more about AmeriCorps*VISTA may call: 1-800-424-8867.

My reasons for writing this book may be described as 'committed' . . . committed to a cause of helping to improve the lives of those less fortunate. If they had not learned from me; I certainly have learned from them; that material things do not bring happiness but true faith in God does. And though they had little in the way of material things, they did have spiritual values. My going to VISTA strengthened my faith in God and made my relationships with other people take on real meaning. Some paths are made to be taken and this was an experience of a lifetime. I would like to recommend to every person to help the less fortunate, if even, just once, in their lifetime. To have the privilege (and I *do* consider it a privilege) to walk the lives of the poor in circumstances they did not choose, will change your life forever.

To have planted pine trees and watched them grow to twenty feet; to have helped a child and/or young person learn they are not alone because someone cared; to have shown the elderly there *are* people who care what happens to them; to have befriended a frightened teenager in her pregnancy who felt the world had dropped out from under her . . . these particular moments and so many others made me aware that God's work *was* truly my own!

It was hard to leave my home and family but what I heard was a call to bear one another's burdens; helping those for whom there *are no* tomorrows.

"If there is something you would so like to do . . . make it a dream and make it come true. Believe that it will with all of your heart . . . believe in it fully right from the start. Feel the success of it, keep it in view . . . make it an intricate real part of you. Never let doubt interfere anywhere . . . . breathe life into it, think about it and care. What happens, you know, is all up to you . . . if you love it enough, your dream will come true!

DID YOU KNOW???

VISTA <u>touched</u> all phases of a community and all age groups!

VISTAs <u>had</u> to be U.S. citizens . . . at least eighteen years of age . . . not take vows of poverty and obedience (but they were going to be poor)!

VISTAs <u>were</u> a part of the <u>O</u>ffice of <u>E</u>conomic <u>O</u>pportunity . . . good doing . . . possessed with America's dis-possessed!

VISTAs <u>worked</u> nine A.M. to nine A.M. Monday through Monday . . . twice as hard as most people . . . for the good of our souls!

VISTAs <u>lived</u> on pennies an hour . . . on love . . . on a desert . . . on an ice floe . . . on a mountain . . . on faith . . . on hope . . . on charity!

VISTAs <u>were</u> . . . <u>V</u>olunteers <u>I</u>n <u>S</u>ervice <u>T</u>o <u>A</u>merica!

Now that you've read through this book, you may be thinking: "Rose seemed to be enjoying a lot of recreation in her VISTA work . . ." (considering we were on call twenty-four hours a day, seven days a week). Visiting an old abandoned gold mine, camping on Shrewsbury Mt. with a group of 4-H girls, attending dances with the natives, blackberrying with Darlene and coming home with empty pails because we saw bear tracks, planting pine trees after the junipers refused to let go of the earth in which they grew, visiting another gold mine with a 'Grand 'ol Patriarch' who knew every tree in those Green Mountains where he grew up and made his home, visiting in my newly-made-friends' homes over pie and tea, and so many times enjoying the streams of the mountains and the moon-rise over those same mountains with Clara, then attempting to find the Big Dipper as it made its appearance in the star-studded sky with Mildred.

These activities all fell in with my attempts to become a member of the community I eventually called home; not to take charge but to help others find a better way of life.

As my thoughts reflect on these writings of God's call to 'bear one another's burdens,' leading me to places I had never dreamed about and finding myself serving Him in new and exciting ways; I give praise and thanks to God for giving me the strength and the courage to assist in the growing needs of others, for whom life was so unfair.

I will continue to go where there is no path and I will leave a trail . . . for the woods *are* lovely, dark and deep, but I have promises to keep and miles to go before I sleep!